Making Money in India

India

I0494765

Business

Guide and

Contacts

By

Patrick W. Nee

The Internationalist

www.internationalist.com

<u>Titles Featured in the Business Guides Series</u>

MAKING MONEY IN CHINA: Key Business
Contacts and Addresses

MAKING MONEY IN CHINA: China Business
Guide and Contacts

MAKING MONEY IN CHINA: China Country
Guide for Businesses

MAKING MONEY IN RUSSIA: Russia Country
Guide for Businesses

MAKING MONEY IN EXPORTING: A
Complete Guide to the Business of Exporting

MAKING MONEY IN Brazil: Brazil Business
Guide and Contacts

<u>**The Internationalist**</u>®

International Business, Investment, and Travel

Published by:
The Internationalist Publishing Company
96 Walter Street/Suite 200
Boston MA 02131, USA
Tel: 617-354-7722
www.internationalist.com
PN@internationalist.com

Welcome to the **Internationalist Business Guides** series:

The key to a successful business is knowing the markets. MAKING MONEY IN INDIA: INDIA BUSINESS GUIDE AND CONTACTS offers executives, investors, and entrepreneurs the need-to-know information about doing business in India.

Written as an in-depth, straightforward reference guide, this book lists key information about the Indian market, its challenges, and opportunities. It then looks into a dozen of India's leading industries, their backgrounds, current situation, and projected course.

Whether you are looking to break into international business or need to update your knowledge on Indian markets— this comprehensive guide is for you.

The Internationalist

Contents

Chapter 1: Doing Business in India

Market Overview

The Republic of India is the third largest Asian economy after China and Japan. Among the major emerging markets, India ranks second in terms of economic growth with the IMF forecasting a GDP growth rate of 6.9 percent for 2012. India is the second most populous country in the world, approximately thirty percent of the country's 1.2 billion inhabitants reside in urban areas. India's industrialized economy encompasses diverse manufacturing sectors (steel production, oil and gas refining, auto, plastics, textiles) while also including traditional village farming, modern agriculture, and handicrafts.

Services, especially information technology, are the major source of economic growth, accounting for more than half of India's output with less than one third of its labor force, which is currently estimated to be 457 million workers. In response to ongoing security concerns, Indian government policies have mitigated terrorist attacks and crime. The increased security presence in urban areas combined with conservative monetary and fiscal policies has allowed India to become one of the more stable economies in the region and thereby lessened the impact of the ongoing global economic downturn.

Moderate inflation of 7.6 percent in 2012, a growing middle class and a relatively stable political environment compared to its neighbors makes India attractive to U.S. companies. India is the United States thirteenth largest trading partner and seventeenth largest import market with total two way trade in goods amounting to approximately $58 billion in 2011. The economy posted an average growth rate of more than 7 percent since 1997, reducing poverty by about 10 percentage points.

Dependent on services exports and private domestic consumption, according to the IMF, India's 2011 GDP registered a 6.8 percent increase reaching USD 1,843 billion with a GDP per capita of USD 3,703. India's 2012 GDP is expected to reach USD 2,072 billion. Multiple factors have affected economic growth in India. They include: the worldwide economic slowdown, an uncertain U.S. recovery, a debt crisis in Europe resulting in a decline in demand in the EU for India's exports, decreasing international financing, and anti-inflationary measures of 2011 introduced by the Indian central bank – the Reserve Bank of India.

Policy uncertainty, stalled reforms, expensive credit and deteriorating political and security conditions are expected to depress economic activity in the short and medium term. The challenging business climate in India attracted only USD 19.42 billion in 2010-11 in Foreign Direct Investment (FDI) falling from $25.83 billion in 2009-2010. Though analysts expected FDI inflows to surpass $40 billion in Indian fiscal year (FY) 2011-12, it stood at $35 billion in April-December 2011, mainly the result of a few large deals. The 2011 nominal exchange rate was 48 Indian rupees per 1 USD and is expected by many economists to fall further against the dollar in 2012. Unemployment reached 9.8 percent; however, more than 60 percent of total employment is in the informal economy.

The government's 15 percent wage hike brought minimum wages in India to USD 130 per month for unskilled workers to USD 160 per month for skilled workers. Rapidly rising salaries with generous perks (cars, housing allowances) have generated high turnover among the professional ranks. The Indian government is promoting public-private partnerships to advance large infrastructure projects and is attempting to diversify its trade beyond Europe and the United States to the Association of Southeast Asian Nations (ASEAN), Latin America, and Africa. Principal U.S. interests run the gamut of industry sectors. Major U.S. companies include: AECOM, Bank of America, Bell Helicopter, Black and Veatch, Coca-Cola, DuPont, Federal Express, General Electric, General Motors, Jacobs Engineering, KFC, Lockheed Martin, McDonalds, Microsoft, Kimberly Clark, PepsiCo, Raytheon, United Airlines, among others.

New FDI reflects well-known hotel brands such as Marriott, Hilton and Hyatt and major engineering firms are pursuing huge infrastructure projects such as the Delhi-Mumbai Industrial Corridor and the Chennai-Bangalore highway project. India's economy is gradually being transformed by India's highly entrepreneurial and rapidly globalizing private sector. Indian firms are investing in infrastructure projects, growing their advanced manufacturing capabilities, and investing in new volume-based business models that tap into rising incomes and consumption in towns and rural economies across the country.

In terms of long-range economic forecasts, major consulting firms project that more than 400 million people, a full 40 percent of the population, will enter India's middle class over the next 15 to 20 years. Given the expected dramatic increase in the size of the Indian middle class, the critical role played by India's private consumption is likely to endure, notwithstanding the Government of India's efforts to become more export-oriented. This "demographic dividend" of India's growing under-35 population is anticipated to be one of the key drivers of long-term growth, provided sufficient employment can be generated. India would like to be viewed as major economy and world power, but it is difficult to overlook that India is home to the largest number of poor people in the world, ranging from 300 million people to 800 million people.

Poor infrastructure, high tariffs and slow pace of economic reforms present the biggest obstacles to foreign investment and growth. India's defense needs and infrastructure requirements also present trade and investment opportunities for U.S. companies. Many large U.S. multinationals are convinced of India's long- term potential and are expanding and deepening their market penetration. U.S. firms with advanced and niche-market products and services are entering the market for the first time, or are replacing legacy distributors appointed in the slow-growth past with more capable and aggressive representatives. Logistics companies are discovering India as a base for distribution throughout Asia. Finally, many smaller American firms have begun to view India as a top anchor market for their products and services as well.

Political and Economic Environment Religion, caste, and language are major determinants of social and political organization in India today. Hindi, the national language, is the most widely spoken, although English is the common language uniting the educated population in a nation with more than 30 major regional languages. Recognizing India as a key to strategic U.S. interests, the United States has sought to strengthen its relationship with India. The two countries are the world's largest democracies, both committed to political freedom protected by representative government. India is also moving gradually toward greater economic freedom.

Market Challenges

Infrastructure: Problems with the country's roads, railroads, ports, airports, education, power grid, and telecommunications are among the toughest obstacles to India's economy growing to its full potential. India's ongoing urbanization, together with rising incomes, have resulted in heightened need for improved infrastructure, both to deliver public services and to sustain economic growth. India is seeking to invest $1 trillion in its infrastructure during the 12th Five-Year Plan (2012-2017) and is looking for private sector participation to fund half of this massive expansion through the Public-Private Partnership (PPP) model.

U.S. companies have been successful in certain areas of India's infrastructure development but competition from other countries is becoming stiffer, and U.S. industry's market share in India in this sector has been declining. Slow Reform Process and Recent Protectionist Policies Even though bilateral trade between our countries has been growing at a steady pace, India has made very little progress in recent years on trade liberalization and in improving market access for U.S. goods and services.

The Government of India (GOI) image was seriously dented in 2011, because of its failure to follow through on pro-reform measures. Import duties continue to be comparatively very high, and exporters and investors are faced with non-transparent and often unpredictable regulatory and tariff regimes. Foreign direct investment rules have been liberalized over time, but many restrictions remain in key sectors, especially in services. The World Bank ranks India among the world's more difficult business climates – 132 out of 183 economies in 2012 (improved from 139/182 in 2011), and next to last in enforcing contracts.

India has embarked on a policy of manufacturing indigenization, with implemented or proposed policies that either ban certain imported products from the market or require some domestic sourcing. In October 2011, the Indian government unveiled the National Manufacturing Policy which encourages government procurement practices that would discriminate against foreign companies. Indian ministries have begun to announce policies that would mandate a certain percentage of domestic content for government contracts. In the last year India has introduced or proposed such requirements in solar energy technology, ICT, and electronic products.

Two long-standing market access concerns that remain stymied are: the flat ban on FDI in multi-brand retail and an increase of the FDI limit on insurance from 26 percent to 49 percent. However, in December 2011, the ruling coalition suspended implementation of its announced intention to open multi-brand retail to 51 percent. Even though the government has reaffirmed its commitment to opening up the multi-brand retail sector and pledged to continue consultations that would permit the rules to be changed, prospects for implementation remain uncertain. Near-term prospects for legislation that would relax insurance FDI rules are also uncertain.

Market Opportunities

Best prospect sectors and business opportunities. These sectors present opportunities for U.S. entrants to the Indian market on the basis of estimated Indian imports from the U.S. for 2012: Architecture, Construction and Engineering Services, (ACE) Civil Aviation Education Services Environment and Water Healthcare and Medical Equipment, Infrastructure (Roads, Ports and Railways), Mining and Mining Equipment, Plastics, Power and Renewable Energy, Travel and Tourism.

In addition to these best prospect sectors there are growing opportunities in the field of homeland security equipment, oil and gas and construction equipment, solar power and food processing and cold storage equipment.

Market Entry Strategy

Strategic planning, due diligence, consistent follow-up, and perhaps most importantly, patience and commitment are all prerequisites to successful business. The Indian sub-continent necessitates multiple marketing efforts that address differing regional opportunities, standards, languages, cultural differences, and levels of economic development. Gaining access to India's markets requires careful analysis of consumer preferences, existing sales channels, and changes in distribution and marketing practices, all of which are continually evolving.

Finding Partners and Agents: New to market businesses must address issues of sales channels, distribution and marketing practices, pricing and labeling, and protection of intellectual property. Relationships and personal meetings with potential agents are extremely important. Due diligence is strongly recommended to ensure that partners are credible and reliable. Geographic Diversity: U.S. companies, particularly small and medium-sized enterprises, should consider approaching India's markets on a local level.

Good localized information is a key to success in such a large and diverse country. The U.S. Commercial Service posts in New Delhi, Mumbai, Chennai, Ahmedabad, Bangalore, Hyderabad and Kolkata provide indispensable local information and advice and are well plugged in with local business and economic leaders. Multiple agents are often required to serve each geographic market in the country.

Market Entry Options: Options include using a subsidiary relationship, a joint venture with an Indian partner, or using a liaison, distributor, project, or branch office.

Chapter 2: Selling U.S. Products and Services

Using an Agent or Distributor

Remember the scale of India and consider a regional approach. Creating a local presence in India is strongly advised, but if your company isn't ready to establish a branch office or a subsidiary, you can get this on-the-ground presence by appointing an agent, representative, or distributor. It's vital to remember that India is a huge and diverse country, with over 30 regional languages. As such, it's strategically important to consider taking a regional approach, and if your product has a wide market appeal, we advise finding regional representatives and distributors.

Defining the Terms: An agent will only procure business and will be paid through a commission. A representative normally works on a retention fee plus a commission on the sales generated. Also, a representative is similar to an indenting agent, where the foreign company deals directly with an Indian importer and then an agent consolidates all the imports, taking a commission from the foreign company. A distributor acts as an importer and typically purchases the product on his own account and stocks the products before selling it to the end user. Due to the risk of stocking the products, the distributor's compensation is higher than that of an agent or a representative.

Use Caution when Establishing Critical Relationship: The Indo-American relationship is strong, and Indian firms are eager to buy American products and services. The market is opening as required by India's WTO commitments, and as a result, U.S.

exporters will find strong interest from potential representatives and distributors for a broad range of products. However, the enthusiasm of potential partners must be weighed against several factors before a relationship is considered. A thorough due diligence study is essential before establishing a relationship, no matter how positive initial meetings are.

When evaluating a distributor or agent, the Indian firm's business reputation, financial resources, willingness and ability to invest, marketing strength, regional coverage, industry expertise, and credit worthiness should be considered. An ideal distributor will have an extremely good banking relationship to enable the extension of credit and also have the capacity to market a full range of products and services. It is important that the agent or distributor have modern infrastructure and facilities such as warehouses, service workshops, showrooms, and trained staff to meet and exceed the expected volume of business.

The Real Gain is in the Growth Market: U.S. companies should be careful not to be influenced by the eagerness and persistence of a distributor or his representative. Sometimes Indian firms represent so many companies that they have little time or interest in developing new markets. The Indian firm may not have the vision to go beyond the existing list of contacts that they have nurtured over time. While in the short run, this can still provide very positive returns, the real edge will be in the areas that are currently underdeveloped. Therefore it is critical to objectively measure the ability, willingness, and aggressiveness of the firm in developing new networks, contacts, and areas of business. By checking multiple professional references, a U.S. company can gain broad insight into an Indian counterpart.

Typical Pitfalls to Expect: The long list syndrome: U.S. companies should exercise pragmatic skepticism when the potential representative offers a long list of foreign clients. These lists may be outdated and the relationships may no longer exist. On the other hand, if all of these relationships do exist, the distributor or agent may not be able to fulfill all obligations and commitments to your product based on the time, financial, managerial, or logistical constraints of building the new relationship. The U.S. companies should confirm that the distributor or agent is able to represent the product along with the products of current clients.

The no follow-through syndrome: U.S. companies should ensure that their distributor or agent is fully committed to promoting their product. Very often the distributors or the agents project a professional image backed by a qualified staff, widespread distribution network and a countrywide presence. The U.S. company should make sure that such representatives do not leave the distribution of their products or services to the network. It is imperative that U.S. companies carefully consider all factors prior to making the final selection of a distributor or agent.

Other issues to Consider: Advantages of a small distributor: A small distributor may be ideal for implementing a flexible distribution strategy. That India is a vast nation of diverse states poses a logistical challenge to a distributor or an agent. A small distributor having presence within a region of India where customers live may be more advantageous, as knowledge of the local market may be a competitive advantage. A small distributor with good product knowledge and marketing skills is often more desirable than a big distributor who leaves the marketing of the product to a section or department of their larger organization. U.S. companies should consider appointing multiple representatives for different products when this is possible.

Due diligence checks: India is a new and rapidly growing economy, and as such, simple and traditional methods of validating the credentials of a potential partner are less reliable, and a thorough due diligence study is critical. Before signing a representative's agreement, a credit check of the proposed partner is imperative. The U.S. firm should check with the distributor or agent's bank to determine the potential partner's financial health, reputation and credit worthiness, and seek additional details from accountants, lawyers, industrial associations, and other sources. For technical products, U.S. companies should also ensure the technical expertise of the distributor, the condition of the facilities, and the experience of the technical staff. Due care should be taken in finalizing the contract details and/or memorandum of understanding.

To identify agents and distributors, U.S. companies can take advantage of the International Partner Search (IPS) and Gold Key Service (GKS) programs offered by the U.S. Commercial Service through its seven offices in India. To assist with due diligence background checks on local agents and distributors,

U.S. companies can take advantage of the Commercial Service's International Company Profile (ICP) service.

Establishing an Office

The most important parameters in choosing a location in India are: (1) physical infrastructure; (2) state government support and flexibility; (3) cost and availability of power; and (4) the law and order situation. Other factors to take into account include labor availability and cost, labor relations and work culture, and proximity to resources and/or markets. In the area of labor law, an employer with more than 100 workers cannot fire them without permission from a government labor commissioner -- something usually impossible to obtain.

Given the shortage of good commercial office space at reasonable prices in major Indian cities, business centers are a viable option for new companies wanting to establish a physical presence. Business centers are facilities that are ready to move in, wired for communications, and air-conditioned. Billing is normally done on a monthly basis. For long-term use, discounts are generally available. Many state governments are creating special Technology Parks for selected industry sectors like software, biotechnology, and automotive.

Type of Office: A foreign company or individual planning to set up business operations in India – but choosing not to establish a subsidiary or to form a joint venture with an Indian partner – can do so by establishing Liaison, Project, or Branch offices in India. Approval from the Reserve Bank of India (RBI) is required, and can be obtained by submitting form "FNC 1" which can be downloaded here. Such companies also have to register themselves with the Registrar of Companies (ROC) within 30 days of setting up a place of business in India.

Liaison or Representative office: Many foreign companies initially establish a presence in India with a liaison or representative office that is not directly engaged in commercial transactions in India. The purpose of these offices is to oversee their networking efforts, promote awareness of products, and to explore further opportunities for business and investment. A liaison office is not allowed to undertake any commercial activity and cannot earn any revenue in India. As no revenue is generated, there are no tax implications to the office in India. Such offices are not allowed to charge any commission or receive other income from Indian customers for providing liaison services. All expenses are to be borne by inward remittances. A foreign company establishing a liaison office cannot repatriate money out of India.

Branch Office: A branch office, like a liaison office, is not an incorporated company but an extension of the foreign company in India. A branch of a foreign company is limited to the following activities by the RBI: representing the parent company and acting as its buying/selling agent; conducting research for the parent company, carrying out import and export trading activities; promoting technical and financial collaborations between Indian and foreign companies, rendering professional or consulting services, rendering services in Information Technology and development of software in India, and rendering technical support to the products supplied by the parent/group companies. A branch office actually does business in India and is subject to taxation in India. The branch office is allowed to repatriate profits generated from their Indian operations to the parent company after paying taxes. However, a branch office is not allowed to carry out manufacturing and processing activities directly (though it can sub-contract such activities to an Indian manufacturer).

Project Office: Foreign companies sometimes set up a temporary project office to undertake projects in India awarded to the parent company. It is essentially a branch office set up for the limited purpose of executing a specific project. Approval for project offices is generally accorded for executing government-supported construction projects or where the projects are financed by Indian and international financial institutions and multilateral organizations. In exceptional cases, approval is also given for private projects. Upon completion of the project, project offices may remit outside India the surplus of the project, after meeting tax liabilities. None of these entities are permitted to acquire real estate without prior RBI approval. However, they are allowed to lease property in India for a maximum period of 5 years.

Franchising

India is witnessing an unprecedented consumption boom. This rapidly growing economy has led to a population of over 300-350 million middle-income Indians with disposable incomes. This group continues to fuel consumption demand in India. The many other factors that contribute to increasing consumption include changing lifestyles of the young urban elite, mounting aspirations, penetration of satellite TV, an increasing appetite for western goods, international exposure, options for quality retail space, and greater product choice and availability.

The greater demand for goods in India is in turn generating a greater demand for franchises. The franchise market in India is estimated to be US$3.3 billion. Franchising in India is growing at an impressive rate of approximately 30%. A recent report by an Indian industry group estimates that over 30 percent of new food outlets, which are coming up in almost all the cities across the country, are established through a franchise system. As many as 17 percent of food and beverage operations in the organized sector are operated by franchisors. At present, there are 1,200 franchisors. Out of which 150 are exclusively dealing in food and beverage retail, 75 percent of which are of Indian origin and rest are international. There are around 18,000 franchised restaurants in the country as compared to only 2,500 run by company owned by these 150 food franchise companies. The report also mentions that education and retail are two important sectors where franchising is prominent. Other important sectors using franchising business model are beauty salons and cosmetics, business services, apparel, education, food and beverage, retailing, tours and travel.

The best prospects for U.S. firms include education and training, food and beverage, health and fitness, beauty salons and supplies, and professional services. Food Franchising: The Indian food franchise sector is on fast-track growth in India. The organized food and beverage retail sector is worth approximately US$280 million and is growing at 25-30 percent annually, with franchises constituting approximately 17% of this growth. Food chains such as Yum Brands, McDonalds, Dominos, and Café Coffee Day have aggressive expansion plans for India. Yum Brands, the parent company of the Kentucky Fried Chicken and Pizza Hut fast-food chains, plans to add 40-60 restaurants in the next 12-18 months. Dominos Pizza India has announced an investment of $55 -58 million in India over the next three years for expanding its retail fast food chain and manufacturing capacities.

Services: Contributing over 50 percent to India's GDP during FY 2011 (April 2010 to March 2011), the services sector holds the key for India's rapid economic growth. Education and training services, professional services, and hospitality services top the list of growing subsectors in the services franchise sector.

Health & Wellness: The $520 million Indian fitness market is growing at 40 percent annually. The Indian population, particularly young Indians, support the demand for personal fitness products. Middle class Indians are increasingly spending their disposable income on spa treatments, health clubs, and wellness programs due to a growing awareness to lifestyle diseases, peer-influence and exposure to media and advertising.

Direct Marketing

Direct selling is a growing industry in India. India ranks 11 in the world in terms of the number of direct sellers. However, when it comes to value of sales, the 14-year old industry in India is ranked 47 . The sales volume recorded by the Indian direct sale industry in 2009-2010 is estimated at $821,535,000 According to industry estimates, there are roughly 20 direct selling companies in India with nation-wide coverage and approximately 100 smaller companies with a localized city specific presence. One Indian firm, RMP, dominates the sector with about half of the sector's gross sales. Many Indian and multinational direct sellers have started operations in India through joint ventures or wholly-owned subsidiaries. Amway, with more than 550,000 active independent Amway business owners spread across over 5,500 locations is the largest direct selling company in India today. It started it operation in India in 2008 and has recorded gross sales of $424,726,000 in 2011, up from $356,929,000.

Tupperware entered India in 1996 and currently has more than 40,000 dealers in 40 Indian cities in 2011 it has recorded growth rate of 52% despite the slowdown of the economy. Established retail companies in India have also started direct selling operations, the most prominent being Hindustan Lever Limited of the Unilever group, Avon Beauty Products India Pvt. Ltd, Amway India Enterprises Pvt. Ltd., Oriflame India Pvt. Ltd. and Mary Kay Cosmetics India Pvt. Ltd. India has strong potential for direct selling because underemployment is perennial. Multinational direct sellers have been quick to sense an opportunity in India's post-liberalization economy.

A key impact made by direct selling activity is visible in the number of Independent Sales Consultants (ISCs) currently participating in the industry. More than 3 million individuals are involved in direct selling activity across India compared to 1.8 million in 2009. Among the ISCs 2.1 million were women indicating the industry's significant role in taking in and empowering women. Product categories include items ranging from health and personal care to kitchenware, education, home care, insurance, and natural products.

For direct selling companies in India with over a billion population of a "word of mouth" advertising is not enough. All leading direct selling brands – Amway, Tupperware, Avon, Oriflame and Modicare are changing marketing strategies in the Indian market and undertaking big advertizing campaigns ion TV, in print and on radio in order to create brand awareness and credibility. More and more direct selling brands are going the celebrity route. Herbalife signed on a cricket player Virat Kohli to endorse its nutritional products. To increase penetration and facilitate direct access to their products, some direct selling companies have also established lifestyle centers and kiosks at major retail stores. A lifestyle store is a large store that carries the entire product range of the marketer but is not meant for retailing. Instead, it is a place for consumers to come and experience the brands and for distributors to conduct their business and impart training. Other direct selling companies set up temporary kiosks at leading retail stores to display and sell their products.

Joint Ventures/Licensing

This type of arrangement is quite common because India encourages foreign collaborations to facilitate capital investments, import of capital goods, and transfer of technology. That aside, India is a market that requires a careful approach because mistakes can be quite costly. Once a decision to go with a joint venture partner is made, it's important to keep in mind the following principles: define each partner's roles and expectations because equality and trust will help keep partners together, experience is a key ingredient, there is no substitute for thorough research, and consider the long term.

There are two channels for foreign investment: the "automatic route" and the "government route". Under the "automatic route", the foreign investor or Indian company is not required to seek approval from the relevant central government agency or department (e.g. coal and lignite mining, power, industrial parks, petroleum and gas, non-banking finance). Instead, the investor is expected to notify the Reserve Bank of India (RBI) of its investment via Form "FC (RBI)" within 30 days of inward receipts and the issuance of shares. Investments subject to government approvals are described as taking the "government route", and approval from vested ministries and agencies is required prior to the investment transaction.

The approving entity varies depending on the applicant and the product. The Ministry of Commerce and Industry's (MOCI) Department of industrial Policy and Promotion (DIPP) oversees single-brand product retailing investment proposals as well as proposals made by Non-Resident Indians (NRIs) and Overseas Corporate Bodies (OCBs). An OCB is an entity that is at least 60 percent owned by NRIs, including overseas trusts. The MOCI's Department of Commerce oversees proposals from export oriented units (i.e., industrial companies that intend to export their entire production of goods and services from India abroad). The Ministry of Finance's foreign Investment Promotion Board (FIPB) oversees all other applications.

The FIPB in the Ministry of Finance is a high-level central agency that deals with and clears proposals for investment in India. The chairman of the Board is the Secretary of the Department of Economic Affairs. Other Board members consist of the Secretaries in the Ministries of Commerce and Industries, and the Economic Relations Secretary in the Ministry of External Affairs.

Other members such as senior government officials and professional experts can be co-opted from government agencies and industry as required. Applications are received by the FIPB. For NRI investment and for investment in the retail sector applications need to be submitted to Secretaries for Industrial Assistance (SIA). The SIA is within the Department of Industrial Policy and Promotion in the Ministry of Commerce and Industry. It provides a single window for entrepreneurial assistance, investor facilitation, processing of all applications that require Government approval, assisting entrepreneurs and investors in setting up projects (including liaison with other organizations and State Governments) and monitoring the implementation of projects.

The timeline for approval for applications made to FIPB and SIA that meet all the required criteria is usually one month. India has taken gradual steps toward FDI liberalization but the process has slowed in recent years. Industrial policy reforms have also stalled. The GOI enacted its National Manufacturing Policy in the fall of 2011. It establishes National Investment and Manufacturing Zones (NIMZ) in an effort to attract FDI. The

National Manufacturing Policy encourages greater local content for government procurement in certain sectors (e.g., ITC, clean energy, solar energy technology, and electronic products). It cites several key priority sectors that could benefit from domestic preferences.

Government approval is required for any foreign investment greater than 24 percent equity when manufacturer is not a small- or micro-sized enterprise (SME) and the entity will manufacture items reserved for SME sector (there are 21 specific goods and services on the reserved list. An SME is a company with total investment in plant and equipment of under $1 million. Manufactures in this category are subject to additional licensing and minimum export requirements. FDI policy is governed by the Foreign Exchange Management Act of 1999 and the RBI.

Investment in the Following Areas are Accorded Priority in Considering Investment Applications: items listed in the automatic approval list, where conditions for automatic approval are not met; infrastructure; items with export potential; projects with large employment potential, particularly in rural areas; items which have a direct or indirect linkage with the agricultural sector; socially relevant projects such as hospitals and life saving drugs; and projects which induct new technology or infuse capital.

If the U.S. investor has written a comprehensive proposal, provided details, and the FIPB is fully satisfied that the investment meets India's industrial development goals, approval can be granted in as little time as three weeks. Proposals that are badly formulated, do not meet FIPB goals, and invite objections on political, environmental or public health or welfare grounds are likely to be denied.

Investment in Existing Pharmaceutical Companies: In October 2011, FDI rules were changed for the pharmaceutical sector. For investments in new projects (green field investments), 100 percent FDI is still allowed. In case of investment in existing companies (brown field investments), FDI will be overseen by the Competition Commission of India (CCI) in accordance with India's competition laws that will ensure a balance between public health concerns and FDI. At the time of this writing no regulations for mergers and acquisitions of the existing pharmaceutical companies have been put in place. This additional government approval requirement is already causing delays for mergers and acquisitions that are currently in the pipeline. Industries Reserved for the Public Sector: Some industries are reserved exclusively for the public sector.

The following industries are not available for private investment unless a specific approval is obtained: arms and ammunition and allied items of defense equipment, defense aircraft and warships, atomic energy, and railway transport.

The need for licensing is attributed to safety, environmental, and defense related considerations. The licensing authority in this case is the Ministry of Industrial Development and the industries are: distillation and brewing of alcoholic drinks; cigars and cigarettes of tobacco and manufactured tobacco substitutes; electronic aerospace and defense equipment of all types;

industrial explosives including detonating and safety fuses, gun powder, nitrocellulose and matches and hazardous chemicals. First Compulsory License to a Patented Pharmaceutical Product: In March 2012 the Controller General of Patents granted a generic drug manufacturer the right to make and sell a generic copy of a Bayer patented cancer drug, citing that Bayer not only charged a price that was unaffordable to most Indians but also did not supply enough doses of the medication to make it available to patients in India. This case was the first compulsory licensing of a patented drug in India and paves the way for a series of similar rulings in the future.

Selling to the Government

The estimated size of the government procurement market at the Central government level in India is about $300 billion and it is expected to grow by more than 10 per cent annually in the coming years. Three sectors -- health including pharmaceuticals, railways, information technology and IT-enabled services represent a large volume of the Indian public procurement market and are expected to grow significantly. Though public procurement accounts for 15 to 20 per cent of Indian economy there is no central law governing the sector.

The situation is similar at the state level. At present only two states -- Karnataka and Tamil Nadu -- have a law governing public procurement. Multiplicity of laws and regulations are implemented by multiple agencies, and Indian government procurement practices and procedures often lack transparency and standardization, which can frustrate foreign suppliers. The process is improving under the influence of fiscal reform policies such those set down in their Defense Procurement Procedure and Manual in 2009 and the revised Defense Procurement Procedure in 2011. Preferences for local suppliers were largely abolished in 1992. Recipients of preferential treatment are now supposedly limited to the small-scale industrial and handicrafts sectors, which represent a very small share of total government procurement.

There are occasional reports of government-owned companies calling in the performance bonds of foreign companies, even when there was no dispute over performance. It is not unusual for negotiations to drag on for months and be held up at more than one of the sundry levels within the Indian bureaucracy for long periods with no discernible movement or reason given for lack of progress. With this in mind some firms seek out local representatives who are familiar with the culture and customs of India, and are familiar with ways to expedite their product or service through the maze of bureaucracy in Government ministries. When foreign financing is involved, principal government procurement agencies tend to follow multilateral development bank requirements for international tenders. However, in other purchases, current procurement practices can result in discrimination against foreign suppliers when goods or services of comparable quality and price are available locally. The Government of India regularly advertises its requirements for the purchase of supplies and new equipment.

Defense Sales: While most of India's defense equipment was previously purchased from non-U.S. sources, India has recently expressed increased interest in U.S. technologies. The Indian defense sales market today offers great potential for defense suppliers, but U.S. businesses desiring to make defense related sales to India should be aware that the process can be a daunting one.

Local Representation is Invaluable: U.S. defense suppliers should assess the merits of having some representation in India to assist in market assessments, logistical support, and after-sales contact. This representation can either be through the supplier's own office presence in India or through an authorized representative. Caution must be exercised when seeking local expertise because unless strict guidelines are followed, Indian law may be broken.

In November 2001, the Government of India lifted the ban on agents in defense purchases. Regulatory provisions were announced for Indian authorized representatives and agents, where permissible, in defense purchases. The regulations require both the principal as well as the potential local representative to meet the provisions stipulated – it is the foreign supplier that has to make an application to the Ministry to register the relationship reached with the agent. The regulations also call for complete disclosure of the principal agent relationship in all its aspects.

The process for gaining clearance from the Government of India (GOI) to hire such a representative can also be very slow. These requirements have discouraged many established local representatives in the defense business from registering as agents for new defense deals. The Office of Defense Cooperation (ODC) within the U.S. Embassy in New Delhi works with the

Commercial Service in New Delhi to assist U.S firms by providing contact details of Ministry of Defense and Military Service offices that are the main purchasers of foreign defense goods for India and offer advice on strategies for defense related sales.

The tender process that the GOI uses to acquire new defense equipment is relatively slow and complex, with the average time between initial release of a request for proposal and the final contract award often taking several years. The most successful firms are those with the endurance to follow the process through and the situational awareness that comes from local representation or from contact with GOI officials. Tenders are generally posted to the Internet, but most U.S. firms will want to establish MOD contacts and understand emerging opportunities and the requirements process well before tenders are publicly accounced. Many ministries announce tenders specific to their ministry on their own website.

Distribution and Sales Channels

There has been a significant expansion in distribution channels in India during the past few years. The size of the Indian retail market in 2011 exceeded $4.9 billion. It is projected that it will grow to $7.1 billion by 2016 averaging 7.5% growth annually. The total number of retail distribution outlets in the country is estimated at over 12 million, mostly family-owned businesses. An annual growth rate for the fast moving consumer goods (FMCG) sector is predicted at 10-12 percent during the next 10 years. A firm can take its products to the user through a variety of channels. It can use different types of marketing intermediaries. It can structure its channel into a single-tier or a three-tier system.

The three-tier system: Most Indian manufacturers use a three-tier selling and distribution structure that has evolved over the years: redistribution stockists, wholesalers and retailers. As an example, a FMCG company operating on an all-India basis could have between 40 and 80 redistribution stockists (RS). The RS will sell the product to between 100 and 450 wholesalers. Finally, both the RS and wholesalers will service between 250,000-750,000 retailers throughout the country. The RS will sell to both large and small retailers in the cities as well as interior parts of India. Depending on how a company chooses to manage and supervise these relationships, its sales staff may vary from 75 to 500 employees. Wholesaling is profitable by maintaining low costs with high turnover, with typical FMCG product margins anywhere from 4-5%. Many wholesalers operate out of wholesale markets. In urban areas, the more enterprising retailers provide credit and home-delivery. Now, with the advent of shopping malls impacting the retail sector, companies talk of direct delivery and discounts for large retail outlets.

Outsourcing logistics: In recent years, there has been increased interest from companies to improve their distribution logistics in an effort to address a fiercely competitive market. This in turn has led to the emergence of independent distribution and logistics agencies to handle this important function. Marketers are increasingly outsourcing some of the key functions in the distribution and logistics areas to courier and logistics companies and searching for more efficient ways to reach the consumer.

The courier network in India now spreads to smaller Class IV towns (defined as towns with populations less than 50,000).

Clearing and Forwarding: Most FMCG and pharmaceutical companies use clearing and forwarding (C&F) agents for distribution and each C&F agent services stocks in an area, typically a state. It is also important to note that duty structures vary among states for the same product, thus creating disparate pricing. But with the introduction of VAT at every stage from producer to end consumer, retail prices are now the same throughout India. With the cost of establishing warehouses extremely high, C&F agents are fast becoming the norm. Recently companies have been utilizing the same distribution channels for products with complementary characteristics.

India has eleven major seaports and 139 minor working ports along its two coasts, but in terms of gross weight tonnage conveyed annually, Mumbai, Marmagao on the west coast, and Vishakhapatnam and Chennai along the east coast are the most important ports in India. Mumbai, the financial capital of the country is very important for the international cargo trade.

Selling Factors/Techniques

At first glance, the bulk of the purchasing power in India would appear to be concentrated in its urban markets. However, a majority of the Indian population lives in rural areas distributed over some 627,000 villages. The balance lives in 3,700 towns of which approximately 300 have a population of more than 100,000 inhabitants. It is said that the real India lives in the villages. All marketers, both Indian and foreign, have benefited by paying attention to the marketing potential of rural India. Analysis of consumer purchase data over the last several years by various research agencies has shown that rural markets in India are growing as disposable income and literacy levels increase, and television access stimulates demand.

Analysts predict that Indian rural consumers worth $100 billion will drive consumption in 2012. Due to the influence of the media, consumption patterns in rural households have also changed significantly in recent years. Indians in rural areas are far more brand conscious, and this is generating demand for some products that were previously unfamiliar. Growing brand awareness makes it all the more important for American companies entering the Indian market to register their brand name with the Indian trademark office. For the country's mega-marketers, rural reach is on the rise. Poor infrastructure, however, is a major problem that makes distribution difficult and reduces demand for some products in rural areas. In order for sales techniques to be successful, distribution coverage is of prime importance.

Indian consumers are serviced by an efficient, but highly fragmented, trade system consisting of over 12 million retail and wholesale outlets, spread over many urban and rural population centers. India has the largest retail outlet density in the world, but the majority of these stores are very small in size and unorganized. With more than 500 million people under the age of 25, India's rapidly growing population appears to present limitless opportunities, but many Indian and foreign companies have discovered that for many product categories, only a fraction of India's 1.2 billion population can be regarded as potential customers.

Many companies have been disappointed with the response to products launched in India over the past few years. Initially, these companies grossly overestimated the depth and size of the Indian market for their products. Projections for the growing Indian middle-class range from 150-200 million but these figures have proven to be off the mark for certain products as marketed to the typical Western middle class consumer. Transposing brands and products from other markets did not work. Suitability and adaptation to Indian preferences and conditions are regarded as a significant benefit to Indian consumers and is therefore an important factor to be considered while designing a sales strategy. A final mistake was to enter India without an efficient distribution network, forgetting that India is a market with poor infrastructure and logistics.

A successful sales strategy will recognize and deal with the existence of strong local competition - this exists in many products and service categories and should not be underestimated. U.S. firms must also carefully compare customer needs and the quality of latent demand with the level of service that they want to offer in India. Even among the affluent middle class, much of their money is spent on need-based consumption rather than on luxury goods. While selling in the Indian market can be a complicated and difficult experience for new entrants, this can be avoided if, at the outset, the market opportunity is assessed accurately and the capabilities of local competition are not underestimated. Only in unusual circumstances should new foreign entrants create a new and independent sales infrastructure, because it is very expensive in the short run, and requires sustained investment to build over the long run, even if the product is successful.

Electronic Commerce

In addition to traditional selling techniques, the Internet is also gaining importance as a selling method. India is now the third largest Internet user base with about 121 million users after China and the US. According to the government India's Internet user base is expected to grow almost six-fold to 700 million by 2014 who would use Internet with shares connections such as cyber cafes, homes and offices. As the number of Internet users continues to increase with the reduction in cost of Internet access, the Indian e-commerce market will also expand.

The latest data from the Internet and Mobil Association of India (IAMAI) estimates the e-commerce turnover was $7.0 billion in 2010, up from $2.8 billion in 2008. The majority of these deals, 80%, are related to booking travel (airways and railways) and hotels, with the remainder in e-tailing, net banking, bill payments, stock trading, job searches, matrimonial searches, general classifieds, online advertisement and online search marketing. The growth in e-commerce is largely due to the increasing number of broadband users. India is expected to have over 175 million broadband connections by 2014. Service providers are upgrading their capacity, but in the short run the supply of broadband is still a cause of concern.

A well-known global technology research firm is upbeat on the potential for online shopping in India. Similarly, industry experts believe that online business-to-business (B2B) commerce will increase substantially in India because it meets a genuine need and portals offering such services are built on strong revenue models.

Trade Promotion and Advertising

Over the years, the Indian economy has moved from being a controlled sellers' market to a buyers' market. With the opening of the economy came increased competition, and the need for increased advertising. Media availability has increased exponentially with unlimited competition. In the year 2011, the Indian advertising industry stood at $5.1 billion, recording a growth of 8 percent. The growth projections for the ad industry by industry experts for 2012 are 8-9 percent, with a total advertising sector of $5.6 billion. Practically every aspect of media is available for advertising, from print to outdoor advertising to satellite channels to movie theaters.

Advertising in print continues to hold the largest share. television advertising dominates the market with a share of 44.8 percent, followed by print with a share of 42.2 percent. Radio saw no growth in 2011 at 3.1 percent share, and outdoor advertising has a 5.1 percent share of the advertising market. The Internet share claims the third largest share of the market at 3.8 percent. A well- known industry consulting group predicts that Internet would become a 5 percent media. The key to gaining rural market share is increased brand awareness, complemented with a wide distribution network. Rural markets are best covered by mass media - India's vast geographical expanse and poor infrastructure pose problems for other media to be really effective. India has a diverse and growing number of daily newspapers.

Print media reaches 70 percent of urban adults. Further, the number of readers in rural India is now roughly equal to that in urban India. The print media, almost completely controlled by the private sector, is well developed and advertising and promotional opportunities are available in a large number of newspapers including daily, weekly or monthly business publications, news magazines and industry-specific magazines. According to the Indian Readership Survey 2011 data The Times of India is the leading English newspaper daily in India, with a readership of 7.4 million, followed by Hindustan Times with 3.6 million. The Economic Times and Business World are the predominant business publications. The top Hindi daily is Dainik Jagran with readership 16 million. The leading magazines include India Today, Business India, Business Today, and Outlook. Advertising opportunities are also available on satellite and cable television channels.

Doordarshan, the government-owned television network, reaches almost 90 percent of the population. In addition, more than 100 satellite and cable television channels, including many U.S. and international channels such as STAR TV, CNN, NBC, Discovery, National Geographic and BBC, are available for advertising. New distribution platforms like Direct-to-Home (DTH) are increasing the subscriber base and raising subscription revenues. Radio, by far the least expensive and most traditional form of mass entertainment in the country, is staging a comeback in the lifestyles of Indians. Presently this medium is dominated by the government-owned

All India Radio (AIR) and reaches over 99 percent of the people in India. Today privately- owned FM radio   stations are present in 90 cities operating on 280 operating frequencies and reach 60 million people. According to an industry body report, FM radio is expected to grow at a CAGR of 16 percent annually and reach a size of $328 million by 2014. New formats such as satellite, internet and community radio have also begun to hit the market.

U.S. companies interested in advertising in Indian media can work through the many advertising agencies in India. Many large and reputable U.S. and other international advertising agencies are present in India in collaboration with local advertising agencies. The advertising sector in India is technologically advanced. In addition to advertising, established public relations firms are also available to U.S. companies that require such services. This segment has a few U.S. and other international companies present in collaboration with local partners. Mumbai remains the center of the advertising industry in India. U.S. companies can select from a number of quality international trade fairs, both industry-specific and horizontal, to display and promote their products and services.

The U.S. Department of Commerce (USDOC) certifies a number of Indian trade shows as good venues for U.S. companies; and the U.S. Commercial Service (CS) offices in India directly organize U.S. participation in a number of selected trade shows every year. Trade development offices of the U.S. Department of Commerce, U.S. industry associations, and individual U.S. states organize trade delegations and missions to visit India to explore prospects for doing business with local firms in the private and public sectors. Participation in such trade missions, whose programs in India are managed by the U.S. Commercial Service, will be useful for American companies interested in doing business in India. The Commercial Service in India offers several easy and inexpensive options to begin promotion in the Indian market, which are particularly helpful to small and medium new-to-market companies. Commercial News USA (CNUSA) is monthly catalog magazine circulated world-wide through U.S. Commercial Service offices with low-cost advertising opportunities; while it's not country-specific, over 3,000 copies are circulated to selected buyers, agents/distributors, chambers of commerce and trade associations in India. U.S. Exporters can arrange for customized services through our Single Company Promotions.

Pricing

When formulating key strategies and making decisions about product pricing for the Indian market, it is important to remember that simple conversion of U.S. dollar prices to Indian rupees will not work in most cases. Also, the assumption that a latent niche market for premium products exists has often resulted in low sales volumes and negligible returns for some foreign companies. If the product can be imitated easily in terms of quality and service, international pricing will not work in India because local entrepreneurs will quickly adopt the same business opportunity. To reduce product import duties or other local costs and ensure a stable market share, several U.S. and other foreign companies have set up product assembly shops in India.

Pricing decisions also have some bearing on product packaging. Many consumer product suppliers have found it helpful to package smaller portions at reduced prices rather than "economy" sizes. Although some Indian consumers are aware of quality differences and insist on world-class products, many customers can sacrifice quality concerns for price reductions Bargaining for the best price is a routine process of the buyer and seller in India. For consumer goods, especially for durables, the sellers often give discounts on the listed prices during festive seasons to attract more customers. Trade-ins of old products for new items are also increasingly popular among consumers. A pricing strategy must consider all of these factors.

Another key consideration in pricing is Indian import tariffs. These are high for most products, especially consumer products. There are pockets of affluent Indians who can afford to buy a variety of luxury branded goods. However, in general, consumer consumption patterns are very different from those in many other countries. The middle class is growing exponentially, providing a fertile market for moderately priced items, but the prohibitive import tariffs may serve to move some items out of the reach of the Indian middle class consumer. Compounding this is the Value Added Tax (VAT) at a rate of 12.5 percent is in effect in most States

Protecting Your Intellectual Property

Indian law at present does not provide for protection against unfair commercial use of test or other data that companies submit to the government in order to obtain marketing approval for their pharmaceutical or agricultural chemical products. Without specific protection against unfair commercial use of clinical test data, companies in India seek immediate government approval for marketing of pharmaceutical and agrochemical products based on the original developer's data. In order to comply with its international obligations under the TRIPS Agreement, the Government of India had designated the Department of Chemicals and Petrochemicals, Ministry of Chemicals and Fertilizers as the responsible ministry to suggest measures that should be adopted in context of Article 39.3 of TRIPS Agreement and to consider whether data protection can be offered under the existing legal provisions.

An Inter-ministerial Committee was constituted on February 10, 2004 under the Chairmanship of Secretary Reddy to act as a Consultative Group on the matter. The Committee released the Reddy Report on May 31, 2007. The Reddy Report finds that the present Indian legal provisions on data protection are not adequate to meet the spirit of Article 39.3 of TRIPS Agreement, though it concludes that existing legislation may be amended to achieve TRIPS consistency. The report further recommends that an explicit legal mechanism in the Drugs and Cosmetics Act, 1940 and the Insecticides Act, 1968, and the Rules framed under these Acts, should be provided to ensure that undisclosed test data of the originator is not put to unfair commercial use by others. The Ministry of Agriculture had drafted the Pesticides

Management Bill, 2008 which includes provisions for data protection for agricultural chemicals and the Bill was introduced in the Parliament on Oct 21, 2008. The Bill was then referred to the Standing Committee on Agriculture for their recommendations.

The Standing Committee's recommended that the term of data protection in the bill be increased from three (3) years to five (5) years. The Ministry of Agriculture amended the Bill in accordance with the Standing Committee's recommendations the amended Bill was to be re-introduced during the Winter 2011 session but could not be taken up and will be re-introduced in the next Parliamentary session. While the Government of India has considered instituting a regulatory data protection system for agrochemicals, there has been little or no movement on providing data protection for pharmaceuticals.

Copyrights: India is a signatory to the Berne Convention and India's Copyright Act of 1957 provides for both civil and criminal penalties for copyright infringement. The Information Technology Act of 2000 includes penalties for the unauthorized copying of computer software. Penalties of up to $240,000 can be applied to unauthorized copying. Also, the penalty affords no immunity from prosecution under other laws. The GOI is not a party to either the 1996 WIPO Copyright Treaty (WCT) or the WIPO Performances and Phonograms Treaty (WPPT).

India is now in the process of considering an amendment to its Copyright Act which includes provisions implementing the WPPT and WCT. The Copyright Amendments Bill was first introduced into Parliament in April 2010 and referred to the Standing Committee on Human Resources Development for evaluation. The Standing Committee submitted its recommendations to Parliament in November 2010 and they were examined by the Ministry of Human Resources Development. The Ministry amended the Bill in accordance with the Standing Committee's recommendations and was planning to introduce the Copyright Amendments Bill during the Winter 2011 session.

The Opposition party was able to prevent the Bill from being taken up and the Ministry will seek to reintroduce the Bill during the next Parliamentary session in 2012. Enforcement of copyright continues to be a problem in India. The Indian Constitution delegates enforcement responsibility to the state governments. The central government can pass laws but the states are responsible for implementing them. The Central Bureau of Investigation (CBI), for example, which has inter-state jurisdiction, does not pursue IPR-related cases. The state, municipal or local police forces - although untrained - are charged with enforcing IPR laws. Piracy of copyrighted materials (particularly software, films, music, popular fiction works and certain textbooks) remains a problem for both U.S. and Indian producers.

India has considered introducing separate optical disc legislation and anti-camcording legislation to address widespread copyright theft but these initiatives have not been implemented. Under existing law, copyright and trademark infringement are characterized as "cognizable offenses" which means that police have expanded search and seizure authority and can make arrests without having a warrant from the court. The law provides for minimum criminal penalties, including mandatory minimum jail terms. Courts rarely impose the full range of penalties prescribed under the law Due to backlogs in the court system and documentary and other procedural requirements, relatively few cases are prosecuted and U.S. and Indian industry report that piracy levels in all sectors remain high.

Cable television piracy also continues to be a significant problem, with estimates of tens of thousands of illegal systems in operation in India. Copyrighted U.S. products are transmitted over this medium without authorization, often using pirated videocassettes, VCDs, or DVDs as source materials. This widespread copyright infringement has a significant detrimental effect on all motion picture market segments in India - theatrical, home video and television. For instance, pirated videos are available in major cities before their local theatrical release.

The proliferation of unregulated cable TV operators has led to cable piracy. The GOI, through the Ministry of Information and Broadcasting, has set up an Anti-piracy Taskforce which was constituted to recommend measures to combat film, video, cable and music piracy in India. The Taskforce issued its report in August 2010 and has made several key recommendations. In its recommendations, the Taskforce has focused on mainstreaming instruments of policy and practice in an effort to make piracy substantially more risky and financially unattractive. The GOI is in the process of examining these recommendations and assessing how they can be implemented.

Trademarks: India's trademark legislation provides protection for trademarks and service marks. A bill amending the Trade Marks Act, 1999 to include provisions relating to the filing of trademark applications under the Madrid Protocol has been cleared by the Parliament. India is expected to formally accede to the Madrid Protocol in the fall of 2012 and begin accepting applications in early 2013. The Intellectual Property Office has also upgraded its IT systems to allow for electronic filing of trademark applications and the Government of India is now considering making e-filing mandatory. Enforcement of trademarks in India's courts is improving and several precedential judgments recognizing the concepts of "well-known or famous marks" and "cross-border reputation" have been issued. The Foreign Exchange Management Act 1999 (FEMA) restricts the use of trademarks by foreign firms unless they invest in India or supply technology. Geographical indications are protected under separate statutory provisions.

Enforcement: India's criminal justice system does not effectively support the protection of intellectual property. India's criminal IPR enforcement regime, including border protection against counterfeit and pirated goods, remains weak. There have been few reported convictions for copyright infringements resulting from raids, including raids against recidivists. Adjudication of cases is slow. Police action against pirates of motion pictures has improved somewhat since 2003. Obstruction of raids, leaks of confidential information, delays in criminal case preparation and the lack of adequately trained officials have further hampered the criminal enforcement process. The GOI has also passed the Drugs and Cosmetics (Amendment) Act, 2008 which enhances the penalties for any adulterated and spurious drugs. The Drugs and Cosmetics (Amendment) Act, 2008 will also create specialized courts to hear cases under the Act. India was considering legislation to establish a special Commercial Division Bench in all of its 21 High Courts which would have jurisdiction over IP disputes. However, this bill was officially withdrawn during the Winter 2011 Parliamentary Session due to problems with its scope and implementation.

IPR enforcement at the border in India is improving. In order to empower Customs Officials to seize goods infringing intellectual property rights at the border without having to obtain an order from the court, Indian Customs Authorities have promulgated the Intellectual Property Rights (Imported Goods) Enforcement Rules, 2007. The Customs authorities have also initiated a records system that will allow rights holders to record their patent, trademark, copyright, design or GI registrations. It will also allow rights holders to request the suspension of clearance of potentially infringing goods. The electronic records system is now available at all ports of entry in India and contains over 400 records. U.S. Patent and Trade Office (USPTO) representatives have an office within the Foreign Commercial Service in the U.S. Embassy in New Delhi that focuses exclusively on intellectual property issues. This office is currently working with the GOI and industry to promote high standards of IP protection and enforcement.

Due Diligence

The U.S. Commercial Service emphasizes the need for exercising prudent procedures and practices in all international business transactions. Every US exporter is advised to conduct a comprehensive due diligence on potential partners in any foreign market to meet obligations under the Foreign Corrupt Practices Act of 1977.

Chapter 3: Leading Commercial Sectors for U.S. Export and Investment

Architecture, Construction, Engineering (ACE) and Construction Equipment

Architecture

The profession and practice of architecture in India has undergone a complete transformation in this decade. The last eight years have been a boom time, not seen since the heady days of Post Independence India. India's skyline is a work in progress. But while the towering new skyscrapers, sprawling IT parks, glitzy airports and swanky townships reflect Indian aspirations, the blueprint, more often than not, is foreign. As Indian developers expand their capabilities and construct and connect new industrial facilities, foreign firms often play a major role in design, construction, engineering and management of various construction projects from airports to residential and office towers, bungalows and resorts.

While presently only architects licensed by Council of Architects (COA) are authorized to practice in India, foreign firms usually pair up with Indian firms to take advantage of the country's real estate boom. According to the Council of Architecture, there are 40,000 registered architects in India, of which only 30,000-odd are practicing - 80 per cent of these in the 10 largest cities. The actual market size is at best a guess as Indian architectural firms do not report their earnings to either the COA or the Indian Institute of Architects (IIA).

This being the case, data on the actual size of this sector is unknown. Most firms are registered as partnership firms and being specialized and highly competitive, do not share much information about themselves, except to highlight notable projects accomplished. Major upcoming opportunities for U.S. firms include the seven technology townships associated with the development of the Delhi Mumbai Industrial Corridor (DMIC). As recently as last year, Godrej hired DP Architects of Singapore to design their 50-storey residential project in Mahalaxmi area of Mumbai. US- based Hellmuth Obata Kassabaum Inc (HOK) has already worked with Indian builders such as Unitech, DLF, Hiranandani and many other big firms.

Obstacles

For an American firm finding the right partner is crucial for gaining a market share in this highly competitive market. There is a general feeling that foreign architects do not understand the complexities of doing business in India, including tax laws and local practices and cultural considerations. A foreign firm who wins a project in India is usually hired for a limited purpose – designing the master plans of the project or concept design, while Indian firms produce the design development and construction documentation and execute the project. Local architects have cost advantage over a foreign firm. Taking the per hour cost of architects based abroad and then pricing the Indian project makes the architect cost prohibitive in many cases.

Additionally, recently with low housing sales and delays in projects architects often do not get paid or at best are forced to accept lower fees for the jobs already performed.

Construction Equipment

The Indian construction machinery and equipment industry is expected to be vibrant due to an increased government focus on infrastructure development. With an estimated $330 million import market, this sector is growing at a rate of 15-20 percent annually. Equipment cost as a part of construction cost ranges from 4.5 percent to 24 percent. Construction accounts for 5.2 percent of the Indian GDP (at constant prices).

Currently, Indian firms manufacture a limited range of construction equipment and only offer services related to the installation and commissioning of the equipment. There are around 200 public and private construction equipment manufacturers in India. These companies mainly produce lower-end construction equipment and offer products from foreign partners to meet the demand for higher capacity and specialized construction equipment. India's access to large capacity equipment and sophisticated technology is maintained through these imports. Reduced import duties and a five-year tax holiday for infrastructure ventures have contributed to the expansion of demand for, and production of, equipment.

The Indian construction industry has noted the US practice of leasing equipment and has begun to follow suit. India's first construction equipment bank, "Quipo", was established in March 2002 for the purpose of leasing high-value multipurpose, specialized and general-purpose infrastructure equipment. Ingersoll Rand of the U.S., along with Indian Infrastructure Equipment Ltd (IIEL) and the IFC, has established an equipment bank in Gurgaon, near New Delhi. They are also developing a second hub, NAC Infra Equipment Ltd (NACIEL), in Hyderabad. NACIEL is a joint venture of the National Academy of Construction with IIEL, L&T Finance Ltd. and Nagarjuna Construction Ltd. Until recently, the GOI's industrial policies only encouraged public sector investment in major industrial and infrastructure ventures.

Now, private engineering and construction firms are allowed to bid for large government projects. This significant policy change has increased the demand for advanced equipment since transportation, urban and housing infrastructure are key areas of construction. New road project initiatives have also increased the demand for construction equipment. The GOI's national plan has placed a high priority on the National Highway Development project which calls for the construction of a Golden Quadrilateral of high capacity, high quality highways linking the four major cities. Those highways, along with major projects designed to develop the East-West and North-South corridors, are intended to help integrate the country.

To augment available resources, the Department of Road Transport and Highways has taken the lead in encouraging private sector participation in road infrastructure projects. At present, 20 National Highways projects costing about $230 million are in different stages of construction. Recently, the GOI announced that 48 new projects costing an estimated $9 billion would be implemented on a Build-Operate-Transfer (BOT) basis.

Sub-Sector Best Prospects

Earth moving equipment

Material preparation equipment

Tunneling and drilling equipment

Road construction equipment

Concrete equipment

Material handling

Opportunities

Attractive investment options are emerging in the following areas: Earthmoving Equipment, Road construction equipment and material handling equipment appear the most attractive product segments, in terms of size and future growth potential. However, the Indian construction equipment market also presents other areas that are nascent, but which have high growth potential like engineering design services, equipment rentals, repair and refurbishing of used equipment, post sales support, R&D Innovation and end-to-end services.

Prospective Buyers: The GOI, state governments, and private firms, both large and small, buy road construction equipment. Project engineering and construction firms such as Gammon India, Ansal Properties, ECC, a division of Larsen and Toubro, Hindustan Construction and Nagarjuna Constructions also buy construction equipment. The new construction equipment banks are currently buying project specific equipment. The leading Indian institutions participating in financing such projects are the

Industrial Credit Investment Corporation of India (ICICI), the Industrial Development Bank of India (IDBI), Infrastructure Leasing and Financial Services (ILFS) and the Housing and Urban Development Corporation (HUDCO).

International multilateral agencies, such as the World Bank and the Asian Development Bank (ADB) have financed infrastructure projects proposed by GOI. Global tenders for capital equipment purchases in India are often backed by credit or loans from international financial institutions like the World Bank, IDA/IFC or US-EXIM Bank. Indian importers of construction equipment normally open an irrevocable Letter of Credit (L/C) payable to the supplier on the presentation of shipping documents to the importer's bank. However, it is important that payment terms are negotiated between the buyer and the seller well before the date of the final agreement.

Civil Aviation

India is the ninth biggest aviation market in the world. In terms of domestic traffic, India is the fourth largest in the world behind U.S., China and Japan. Despite these numbers, India is one of the least penetrated air markets in the world (even lower than Sri Lanka, Pakistan and Nigeria) with 0.02 trips per capita as compared to 0.2 of China and 2.2 in the U.S. This reflects significant potential for future growth. The Indian aerospace sector ranks among the world's most dynamic.

Boeing estimates that India will spend $130 billion to purchase 1150 aircraft over 2030. India has a total of 128 airports out of which 15 are international airports, 8 are custom airports with limited international operations, 80 domestic airports and 25 are civil enclaves in defense airfields. The Airports Authority of India (AAI) manages all the airports except Delhi, Mumbai, Hyderabad, Cochin and Nagpur, which are managed under public private partnership (PPP) framework.

The AAI controls India's of about 2.8 million nautical square miles area. The AAI develops and manages airports and also provides air traffic management services and air infrastructure. The traffic at India Airports has increased at a rate of 15.3% over last 9 years – primarily led by high growth in domestic traffic. In year 2010-2011 passenger air traffic reached 143.3 million, and during the same period Indian airports handled 2.3 million MT tons of cargo. Starting from a relatively small base, the civil aviation sector in India faces the prospect of significant expansion as the overall economy recovers and India retains the second-highest growth rate worldwide.

Market Size

For a country of more than one billion people with a sizeable middle class (200-250 million) that can afford air travel, the size of the aviation sector is relatively small. While the U.S. has on average 50,000 commercial scheduled aircraft movements per day, India has a little over 3,800 each day. Furthermore, much of the traffic flow is located in the five major cities of the country: Mumbai in the West; Delhi in the North; Bangalore and Chennai (Madras) in the South; and Kolkata (Calcutta) in the East. India is ideally positioned as a major aviation hub at the crossroads between Europe, the Middle East and Asia Pacific.

The fact that aviation was a neglected sector for so long has allowed airports such as Dubai and Singapore to effectively establish themselves as offshore hubs for Indian passengers, and they now have a significant head start. However, as India's airports improve, and its airlines receive international awards for their service, there may be an opportunity to leverage its huge home market to compete with these longer established hubs. India has been successful in modernizing its largest airports through PPP with foreign participation – Delhi, Mumbai, Bangalore, Hyderabad and Cochin. Expansion is underway at other major airports – Chennai and Kolkata.

The Hyderabad International Airport has been ranked amongst the world's top five in the annual Airport Service Quality (ASQ) passenger survey along with airports at Seoul, Singapore, Hong Kong and Beijing. The Hyderabad International Airport is managed by a public-private joint venture consisting of the GMR Group, Malaysia Airports Holdings Berhad and both the State Government of Andhra Pradesh and Airport Authority of India (AAI). Maintenance, Repair and Overhaul (MRO) opportunities exist for servicing 1,000 commercial aircraft and 500 GA aircraft. MRO facilities are also expected to need additional ground support equipment.

Both Boeing and Airbus have decided to invest in a MRO facility. Industry sources estimate that establishing a world class MRO will require an investment of over $250 million. MRO business is estimated to grow at 10% annually and reach $1.2 billion by 2013 and $2.4 billion by 2020. Airlines in India currently outsource major checks and aircraft servicing to MRO hubs like Singapore, Malaysia and Dubai. Worldwide trends exhibit the gradual move towards third party MROs. Nearly 50% of US based airlines maintenance is outsourced to MROs and 45% of military maintenance is outsourced to civilian MROs. Both government and private players have evidenced keen interest in this area with the intention of providing reliable and cost-effective maintenance services to all Indian carriers.

The aerospace sector in India is in the early stages of development and most of the domestic demand is being met through imports. Hence, opportunities for the American Aviation companies in the Indian Aviation Aerospace industry are abundant in the area of technology, raw material development capabilities, international airworthiness certifications, developing skills, providing financing, etc. The present market size for airport and ground support equipment is estimated to be $440 million. Successful privatization of airport maintenance and ground support services will lead to another $100 million in market growth over the next three years.

The most promising sub-sectors in the airport equipment and ground-handling services continue to be technology-driven communication and ground services. The AAI (airport Authority of India) has an annual budget of approximately $100 million for procurement of equipment that are dependent on foreign technology.

Airport Growth Beyond Metro Areas
To ensure that the development of the sector was not restricted to the metro cities alone, the GOI announced its plans to modernize

35 non-metro airports into world-class entities at an estimated cost of $1.2 billion. The airports to be modernized include Coimbatore, Tiruchi, Thiruvananthapuram, Visakhapatnam, Port Blair, Mangalore, Agatti, and Pune. The Ministry of Civil Aviation has also approved greenfield airports at Navi Mumbai, Goa, Durgapur, Kannur, and Saras.

Upcoming Opportunities

Investment opportunities of $ 110 billion are being envisaged up to 2020 with $80 billion in new aircraft and $ 30 billion in development of airport infrastructure, according to the Investment Commission of India. The Indian Ministry of Civil Aviation is also addressing other important issues that will result in long-to- medium term opportunities for U.S. companies. These opportunities include decreasing the systematic cost in the sector and determining the appropriate mechanism for providing air services to remote and commercially unviable sectors as part of a comprehensive long-term civil aviation policy. The Airport Economic Regulatory Authority (AERA) Bill was passed by the Indian Parliament to ensure that India's aviation infrastructure meets cost, efficiency, and service targets by making policies consistent with the International Civil Aviation Organization (ICAO) standards.

U.S. – India Relations in Civil Aviation

U.S. – India relations in civil aviation are at an all-time high with regular exchanges at the highest levels by respective governments. U.S. exports of civil aviation equipment and services comprise over 15 percent of total U.S. exports to India. The Ministry of Civil Aviation and the Federal Aviation

Authority (FAA) of the United States meet regularly through the Joint Aviation Steering Committee. FAA also maintains an office at the American Embassy in New Delhi. In 2007, The U.S. and India Aviation Cooperation Program (ACP) was established at the initiative of the Department of Transportation and the Ministry of Civil Aviation. The ACP is a Public Private Partnership (PPP) between the U.S. Federal Aviation Administration (FAA), the U.S. Trade and Development Agency (USTDA), U.S. Commercial Service, U.S. companies, and the Government of India. U.S. companies are encouraged to be a member of ACP to better explore and exploit opportunities in the Indian civil aviation sector.

In 2010, civil aviation was added as a new sub-committee under the High Technology Cooperation Group (HTCG). The HTCG was constituted in 2002 and provides a forum for the two governments to promote and facilitate bilateral commerce in high technology sectors, including Defense and Strategic Trade, Biotechnology, and Nanotechnology. The sub-committee meets periodically under the leadership of U.S. Department of Commerce A/S Lamb-Hale and Indian Civil Aviation Secretary Zaidi to discuss mutual areas of cooperation in airport infrastructure.

Education Services

India has one of the largest and oldest systems of higher education. Presently, there are 496 universities in the country, including 239 state universities (established by the state governments), 130 deemed universities (a status of autonomy granted to high performing institutes and universities by the

Department of Higher Education), 40 central universities (established by the Department of Higher Education), 49 private universities, and 38 institutes of national importance, such as Indian Institute of Technology (IIT), and Indian Institute of Management (IIM). In addition, there are private and accredited universities, institutions created by an act of Parliament, independent institutes and over 16,000 colleges. Together they offer a wide range of degree and diploma programs. Secondary education is growing significantly in India due to both government and private sector participation. It is seen as the backbone of further education initiatives in India.

The Government has started programs to ensure continual supply of students for higher education programs. Over the past decade the number of students going for their undergraduate programs and advanced programs has increased significantly. Higher education in India is regulated by the University Grants Commission (UGC), All India Council of Technical Education (AICTE) and other councils established under applicable statutes for the regulation of education in specific fields. Some of the councils and the specific fields that they govern include Council of Architecture, Pharmacy Council of India, Indian Nursing Council, Medical Council of India, Distance Education Council etc. Higher education institutions operating in India for at least 10 years can be conferred with a special status of 'deemed universities' (DUs) upon satisfying prescribed criteria. DUs have degree granting powers. AICTE is also the nodal body regulating the entry and operation of foreign universities / institutions in India.

Market Data

Higher education has been accorded high priority status in India, especially in the past few years. The Government of India (GOI) aims to increase gross enrollment ratio in higher education to 30% by 2020, which means almost tripling the enrollment from present 14 million to 40 million at a CAGR of 12.8%. And this target would be achieved by expanding existing institutions and establishing new institutions and universities. It is estimated that education is the third largest expenditure group for an average Indian family. Currently, the Indian population in the relevant age group enrolled into higher education courses is more than that of Europe, USA, Australia combined.

It is generally acknowledged that despite the quantity of schools, the quality of education varies widely among Indian institutions. To meet the needs and to prepare its large youth population for tomorrow's careers, India does not have sufficient capacity to meet the demand. If India is to meet its goals, an additional 1,000 universities and 50,000 colleges are needed. This offers tremendous opportunities for US institutions to participate in this sector and build capacity. United States - The chosen destination: Indian students and their parents strongly believe that higher education in the United States prepares graduates for careers of tomorrow. More than half of all Indian students studying overseas choose U.S. universities.

The attraction of a U.S. education can be attributed to: Variety and flexibility of the U.S. education system Grounding in practical and career-focused training Career opportunities in India post graduation India is primarily a "graduate market" for

U.S. institutions interested in attracting students. Though there is some interest in U.S. undergraduate studies and transfer admissions, limited scholarships and the increasing cost of education are major deterrents. However, with the mushrooming of international schools in the country and the return of many U.S. citizen children born to Indian American parents to India, we anticipate an increase in interest in undergraduate study in the years to come. India has a severe shortage of higher education institutions for its booming population where more than 30% of its 1.1 billion people are less than 14 years old. This trend creates a large demand for higher education in near future.

The United States, with over 6,000 accredited institutions of higher learning, has the capacity to offer access to high quality education to students in a broad range of fields. Employers in India have stressed the importance of a workforce equipped with adequate technical, teamwork and communications skills. In the 20010/11 academic year, 103,895 students from India were studying in the United States (down 1% from the previous year). India is the second leading place of origin for students coming to the United States.

Competition for U.S. Schools from other countries: Although the United States remains the first choice for Indian students studying abroad for the past few years, American institutions have been losing significant market share to rivals from other countries, especially the United Kingdom and Australia. The United Kingdom, Australia, Canada and New Zealand have been aggressively promoting their programs in India. They have been actively participating in many education fairs and fully utilizing local education consultants as their marketing representatives to recruit students.

Opportunities

India offers substantial opportunities for U.S. universities and other institutions of higher learning to establish schools, programs and curriculum in India. Experts estimate the Indian education market at a potential value of $28 billion. Obama-Singh 21st Century Knowledge Initiative: The Obama-Singh 21st Century Knowledge Initiative, launched by U.S. President Barack Obama and Indian Prime Minister Manmohan Singh, creates a path for higher education partnerships between US and Indian institutions. Both the Governments have pledged US $ 5 million for this endeavor which will fund University linkages and Junior Faculty Development. A Joint Working Group (JWG) with three members each from the USA and India has been constituted for implementation.

The program has the following broad components:
- Faculty Development
- Academic Leadership Programs
- Development of Community Colleges
- Enhancing Institutional Linkages

Foreign Education Institutions Bill: The Foreign Education Institutions (Regulation of Entry and Operations) Bill 2010 is being assessed in the Parliament. According to the provisions of the Bill, any foreign varsity entering India will have to create a $12 million corpus fund. Excerpts from the draft bill: 'A foreign education provider shall, out of the income received from the corpus fund, utilize not more than seventy-five per cent of such income for the purposes of development of its institution in India and the remaining of such unutilized income shall be deposited into the corpus fund. No part of the surplus in revenue generated in India by such Foreign Education Provider, after meeting all expenditure in regard to its operations in India, shall be invested for any purpose other than for the growth and development of the educational institutions established by it in India.

A foreign education provider shall ensure that the course or program of study offered and imparted by it in India is, in conformity with the standards laid down by the statutory authority, and is of quality comparable, as to the curriculum, methods of imparting education and the faculty employed or engaged to impart education, to those offered by it to students enrolled in its main campus in the country in which such institution is established or incorporated.' Foreign universities, however, will have the right to form their own fee structure and admission rules. Though 100% FDI is allowed in education sector, the current legal structure in India does not allow granting degrees by foreign educational institutions. With the introduction of the Bill, foreign education providers will be allowed to set up campuses in the country – independently or jointly and offer degrees.

Environment/ Water

Overview

It is estimated that 30-40 percent of India's industrial units produce sizeable quantities of pollutants. There are about 3 million small-scale units in the country and most of these are not using any pollution control equipment. The Government of India has classified 17 industrial sectors as strong pollutants. India is one of the largest and one of the fastest growing producers of greenhouse gases. India's pollution control equipment industry is growing at 10-12 percent annually, largely because of government initiatives and a proactive judiciary. Local production is mainly into standard, low-tech equipment. Forty percent of market demand is met by imports. Germany, UK, Japan, Canada, Australia, Netherlands, and Italy are among the major suppliers. The United States is the market leader for imports, having over 30percent of market share.

Until recently, the environmental goods & services sector used to refer to solutions for air, noise & marine pollution, land & water contamination, environmental analysis & consultancy, waste management and recycling. Now it also includes renewable energy technologies such as hydro, wave & tidal power, geothermal, wind & biomass, and emerging low-carbon activities like reduced emissions from the transport & construction sector, nuclear energy, energy management, carbon capture & storage and carbon finance. Some of the important environment sectors include: Water Supply & Waste Water Treatment; Solid Waste Management; Air & Noise Pollution; Environmental Goods & Services; Renewable Energy, and Clean Development Mechanism and Carbon abatement technologies.

Market Data

The total market size is estimated to be over $6 billion, with Renewable and Energy Efficiency Indian pollution control equipment industry is unorganized and dominated by small-scale industrial firms lacking the resources to invest in research and development. There are a few medium and large Indian engineering companies offering services and equipment as part of turnkey consulting services. The Ministry of Environment and Forest governs this sub sector and it has allocated a budget of over $300 million for pollution abatement. The market is not restricted to the government sector.

The private sector has been investing substantially in environmentally friendly production processes and accounts for nearly 40 percent of demand in this segment. Poor enforcement of environmental laws is a key reason for the low market potential compared to developed countries. Imports constitute nearly 40 percent of the total market share due to two main factors: Unlike other sectors, multi-lateral and bi-lateral agreements on ecology and the environment play a major role in this sector. This results in an increased demand for imported pollution control equipment, because donor-led investments normally require international quality equipment that is not manufactured in India.

Multinational corporations with manufacturing facilities in India insist on the replication of technology for pollution control. This almost always requires imports. The United States has traditionally enjoyed a dominant position in the market, with over 30 percent of market share. In some segments such as air pollution control equipment, imports from the United States constitute almost 40 percent of total imports. Industry sources believe that the import market will continue to increase and the domestic market share will decline due to increasing demand for improved and innovative technologies that cannot be met by domestic suppliers. Currently it is estimated about 40 percent of total market demand is met by imports.

Sub-Sector Best Prospects

Private sector demand is growing for increased energy efficiency and renewable energy, vehicular and industrial air pollution control, bio-medical waste disposal, and water-recycling technologies. India has a large potential in renewable energy (RE) segment. In addition, there is a huge potential market for generating power, and thermal applications using solar, wind and biomass energy. Exploitation of geothermal energy, tidal energy and bio-fuels for automotive applications is also envisioned. Strict enforcement and implementation of even a fraction of the suggested measures in the National Environment Policy of 2004 would create a huge opportunity for international players in this sector. In addition, major investments will be required by the automobile industry to comply with Euro IV norms in India's 11 largest cities, where vehicle numbers are increasing and overall vehicular pollution is worsening.

Healthcare and Medical Equipment

Overview The Indian healthcare industry is experiencing a rapid transformation. According to the World Health Report, India spends about 5.5 percent of its Gross Domestic Product (GDP) on the healthcare sector. About 50 percent is spent on curative and primary care and another 40 percent on secondary care, including medical specialists in major hospitals with expensive diagnostic equipment. The remaining 10 percent of the market is left to preventive care such as health education, weight reduction plans, and similar programs. The Indian healthcare market is currently estimated at US$56 billion. It is expected to reach US$ 80 billion in 2012 and US$ 280 billion by 2020 according to a report by an industry body. Rising income levels and a growing elderly population are all factors that are driving this growth. In addition, changing demographics, disease profiles and the shift from chronic to lifestyle diseases in the country has led to increased spending on healthcare delivery.

Medical infrastructure in India is far from adequate with demand for hospitals and beds far surpassing availability. India has just one hospital bed for 1,000 patients. A global consulting firm estimates that India needs 1.75 million beds by 2025. The problem is most acute in rural India, which accounts for over half of India's population while about 80 percent of available hospital beds are located in the urban centers, leaving only 20 percent for the larger rural population. Both government and the private sector have strived to bring about rapid growth in the industry to manage the demand for high quality service. This has also brought a surge in demand for high-end medical devices and equipment. Import incidence is high – almost 70 percent of medical equipment for private hospitals is imported. Peak import duties have been lowered to bring India in line with WTO norms.

The boom in medical tourism in the Indian healthcare sector is encouraging hospitals and hoteliers to strike alliances with each other. The cost of most major surgeries in India is much less than the cost for the same surgery in a developed economy. The market size of medical tourism in India, which is growing at over 25 per cent annually, is pegged at over US$ 2.5 billion, according to industry estimates. The healthcare industry is now proactively creating standards for the medical tourism industry with the help of credit rating agencies, insurance companies and others involved in the self-regulation of the sector.

Sub-Sector Best Prospects

The most promising sub-sectors in the healthcare and medical equipment sector are:

Medical Infrastructure

Medical and Surgical Instruments

Medical Imaging

Electro Medical Equipment

Orthopedic and Prosthetic Appliances

Cancer diagnostic

Ophthalmic Instruments and Appliances

Opportunities

In India, healthcare is provided through primary care facilities, secondary and tertiary care hospitals. While the first two categories are fully managed by the government it is the tertiary care hospitals that are owned and managed either by the government or private sector. The private sector's contribution to healthcare has been growing at a faster pace than government.

The medical infrastructure market is estimated at a growth rate of 15 percent. Both the government and private sector are planning several new specialty and super- specialty hospital facilities, as well as up-gradation of existing hospitals. Indian healthcare is also witnessing a public-private partnership for up gradation of government healthcare facilities. Opportunity also exists for overseas organizations to set up hospitals in India through Foreign Direct Investment (FDI) route. The new specialty and super-specialty hospital facilities depend on the import of high-end medical equipment, accounting for over 70 percent of the entire market. Building, equipping and managing super specialty hospitals is another area for future growth.

There is a need for sophisticated hospital equipment, especially operation theatre products. In view of the relatively low customs duty rates (9.2 – 15 percent) combined with an increasing number of healthcare centers specializing in advance surgery, India offers opportunities for the direct supply of high-technology, specialized medical equipment, products and systems. A proper supply of equipment and medical consumables will also be an area with significant opportunity for American companies. Several leading U.S. purveyors of hospital equipment and supplies have opened Indian operations to cater to this growing market.

Health insurance and hospital administration is another area in which U.S. companies can make a difference. This opportunity includes introducing and maintaining industry standards, and also classifying and certifying healthcare centers. Other growth areas include diagnostic kits, reagents and hand-held diagnostic equipment. Imports constitute 50 percent of this market. Hand-held/portable diagnostic equipment (e.g. for blood sugar, blood pressure testing etc) is also a fast growing segment since India has around 45 million diabetics. E-healthcare/Telemedicine though is in its infancy in India, it is beginning to take root. Most public hospitals (funded by State governments) and private single and multi super specialty hospitals have gone in for customized Hospital Management Systems and other medical based IT products. Given the poor availability of quality healthcare facilities outside the large and second tier cities, telemedicine is expected to become viable business proposition.

Infrastructure (Roads, Ports, Railways)

Overview

It is generally recognized that lack of infrastructure is a major constraint to India's economic development. The Government of India's biggest mission today is to improve roads, highways, ports, airports and increase energy production. India is seeking to invest $1 trillion in infrastructure during the 12th Five-Year Plan (2012- 2017) and is looking for private sector participation to fund half of this massive expansion through the Public- Private Partnership (PPP) model.

The Cabinet Committee on Infrastructure (CCI), under the Chairmanship of the Prime Minister, was constituted on July 6, 2009. The CCI approves and reviews policies and monitors implementation of programs and projects across infrastructure sectors. India is one of the world's fastest growing economies and presents exciting opportunities for U.S. companies that offer products and services that can assist in meeting the rapidly expanding infrastructure needs. The rapid growth of the Indian economy (averaging 8% over the past 10 years) has created a pressing need for Infrastructure development and the country needs significant outside expertise to meet its ambitious targets. U.S. industry is well qualified to supply the kinds of architectural, design and engineering services and project management skills needed to successfully tackle major projects, including such groundbreaking projects as the Delhi-Mumbai Industrial Corridor (DMIC). U.S. technologies are also well positioned to rationalize energy use and production to support new industrial zones as they are built in this chronically energy deficit country.

Road/Highways: With a total of 3.14 million kilometers of roads, India has the 2nd largest road system in the world only after the U.S. The National (Interstate) Highways constitute 70,000 kilometers of roads and India intends to double this network in the next 5 years. Additionally, it also intends to increase the overall road network to 5 million kilometers in the next decade, connecting all parts of the country with each other. The Government of India's Planning Commission recently estimated that India will mobilize over $42 billion on spending for roads and related infrastructure over the next several years.

These funds are to be utilized to:
Upgrade and expand the state highway network in the different states of India (to be funded by the Asian
Development Bank);
The Municipal Corporation of Delhi plans to spend $1.24 billion for upgrading the City of Delhi's roads and
infrastructure (as are other big cities);
National Highway projects worth approximately $24.65 billion will be executed in the country connecting the freight corridors running from North-South and East-West to the interior;

Set up related infrastructure – toll booths, warehousing facilities, connector and feeder lanes, etc. to the highway systems.

The Government of India is also formulating regulatory changes to the awarding process and concession agreements to attract more participation from private and foreign developers. Railways: A lifeline to the nation, Indian Railways has the 2 largest railroad network in the world and is the largest employer in India today. Indian Railways has embarked upon a massive restructuring and expansion program over the next decade to modernize the existing network and add new lines.

It's estimated that in the 12th five year plan (2012- 2017), Indian Railways will spend about $67 billion on the following:
Building new routes including Dedicated Freight Corridors (DFC) with Public-Private Partnership (PPP) sub-projects envisaging more than $7 billion investment for the North South, East West corridors alone;
Enhancing container operations; Setting up of rail side warehousing facilities and developing logistics parks;
Developing rail links to existing and new ports with dedicated rail links for evacuation of specific industrial items; and
Modernization of railway stations and systems including rolling stock.

Ports: In the next five years, Indian government will invest $66 billion in the port sector and $27 billion in the shipping sector. The Port sector is a high priority for Government of India and it is encouraging private sector participation in the port development. For the ambitious capacity expansion projects, government has identified Public-Private-Partnership as the preferred mode of attracting investments. FDI in ports are permitted under the automatic route up to 100%. The capacity of the ports during January to December 2011 rose from one billion metric tons to 1.16 billion metric tons. While coastal shipping accounts for about 40 per cent of trade volume in U.S., China and Europe, it is only seven per cent of India's total domestic cargo transport network and there is a scope for development in the sector. The bilateral trade between India and US in merchandise goods increased from $49 billion in 2010 to $58 billion to 2011. Other than Port development and equipment supply there is adequate scope for Indian and American Maritime training institutions to work in collaboration to produce quality maritime human resources.

Sub-Sector Best Prospects

Construction Equipment

Road laying material and chemicals

Railway equipment, technology

Ports equipment,

Maritime technology

Opportunities

The Government of India envisages one trillion dollar investment in all areas of infrastructure in the 12th five year plan (year 2012 to 2017). The Government wants fifty percent of this investment to come from the private sector participation and most of these projects are expected to utilize the Private – Public partnership (PPP) model. The Secretariat for Infrastructure in the Planning Commission is involved in initiating policies that would ensure time-bound creation of world class infrastructure delivering services matching international standards, developing structures that maximize the role of PPPs and monitoring progress of key infrastructure projects to ensure that established targets are realized.

Mining & Mineral Processing Equipment

Overview

India is endowed with significant mineral resources. The country produces 87 minerals and has approximately 2,628 operational mines. India ranks among the top ten global producers for the following metallic minerals: mica, barites, coal & lignite, iron ore, chromite, bauxite and manganese. India's mining sector employs over a million people. The value of mineral production in India from April 2010-March 2011, excluding atomic minerals, was approximately $40 billion, with growth estimated at 11.8 percent over the previous year. Coal, excavated from 570 mines, accounts for a major part of the mining activity.

India ranks third in worldwide production (573.42 million MT in 2010-11) and consumption (656.3 million MT in 2010-11) of coal and lignite. Coal accounts for approximately 52 percent of the country's energy needs. Annual demand for coal is projected to be over 2 billion MT by 2032. The country has a potential coal- bearing area of approximately 17,303 sq. kilometers, of which only about half has been partially explored. India's Investment Commission estimates that investment opportunities, valued at $30-40 billion, will be available over the next ten years to explore and develop new coal mines, manufacture and sell state-of-the- art mining equipment and technology, and to create related infrastructure for the off-take of mined coal.

Sustaining the high growth of the Indian economy will depend on the accelerated pace of growth in the mining of coal and other minerals. However, the mining sector is estimated to record a negative growth of 2.2 percent during the period April 2011-March 2012, primarily due to restrictions imposed on export-driven unregulated iron ore mining and environmental concerns holding up expansion of open-pit coal mining areas. The new Mines and Minerals (Development and Regulation) Bill (2011) seeks a complete and holistic reform in the mining sector with provisions to address issues relating to sustainable mining and local area development.

The Indian market for mining and mineral processing equipment is estimated at over $3 billion. Eighty percent of this is in the coal mining sector. Opencast mines contribute 88 percent of the total production, but there is a renewed focus on underground mining. A number of large opencast mines, those with more than 10 million MT per annum capacity, are in operation. With the focus on increased productivity and private investment in mining, India is expected to become a major market for advanced mining equipment and technology from the United States and other foreign countries including Australia and Germany. A few large manufacturers in each product segment dominate the mining equipment industry. Most of the global technology leaders are present in India as joint venture companies, or have set up their own manufacturing facilities, or marketing companies.

The industry has made substantial investments in the recent past to set up manufacturing bases. Among Indian companies, Bharat Earth Movers Limited (BEML) is the largest and has licensing agreement with international collaborators. Over 100 mining equipment companies operate in India. Although the country has a fairly large domestic manufacturing base, the demand for direct imports of advanced equipment and technology is growing, particularly in coal mining. Government owned mining companies are the biggest buyers. Moreover, the large domestic manufacturers have foreign licensing agreements, which allow indirect import of the critical components for local assembly and incorporation in the indigenous equipment.

There is also an opportunity to directly participate in the mining services market, through operating coal beneficiation plants as well as new or abandoned underground mines on contract. The demand for such services is particularly high for the new coal block lessees in the private sector. There is also a growing market for clean coal technology, such as coal bed methane extraction, coal gasification and coal to liquid projects. Ancillary services such as water and air pollution and hazardous waste management, as well as consulting for acquisition of mines in foreign countries provide additional opportunities. Given the recently liberalized Mineral Policy of the government, and with private entrepreneurs investing in mining industry here, the opportunity for U.S. firms to enter the Indian market through joint ventures, technical collaborations and operating leases has grown immensely.

Government-owned mines contribute 75 percent of the total value of mineral production. In the last decade, however, the economy has been liberalized, tariffs lowered, state enterprises privatized and the country opened to investment in mineral exploration. It is the avowed policy of the Government to withdraw from the non-strategic sectors. Accordingly, public sector undertakings are being privatized gradually. In the iron ore sector, the second largest mineral mined in India in terms of quantity, 70 percent of the mining is done by private sector. Likewise, private investment, including foreign direct investment, is being allowed to mine and process most minerals.

India now allows 100 percent foreign direct investment (FDI) in mining and exploration of non-core minerals like gold, silver, and diamonds. One hundred percent FDI is also permitted in oil exploration and captive mining of coal and lignite. Fifty percent FDI is permitted under joint venture with a public-sector unit. In coal processing (washing and sizing), 100 percent FDI is allowed. Over 200 coal blocks have been allocated to various end-users. Of these, approximately 28 blocks have started production. Total production from captive mines in 2011 was approximately 38 million MT.

Sub-Sector Best Prospects

Coal India (CIL), a large government-owned conglomerate, plans to significantly enhance its production and productivity in the next five years. It is expected to invest heavily in large and specialized mining equipment and services. In keeping with the current emphasis on clean energy options, India will also purchase coal beneficiation, underground coal gasification, coal to liquid, coal bed methane and coal mine methane technologies. Services such as geophysical surveys on coal seams and consulting for acquisition of new mines at international locations will be in demand. In addition to new equipment, some of India's private developers of mines are also interested in exploring the possibility of getting used or reconditioned equipment at a reasonable cost.

There is a strong interest in joint ventures with large, international mine operators to explore virgin mines in India. CIL mines more than 80 percent of India's coal reserves. Along with its eight subsidiaries, it is the largest buyer of coal mining equipment in the country. CIL runs a large fleet of nearly 6000 heavy earthmoving machineries (HEMM), including 41 draglines, 670 shovels, 3200 dump trucks, 1000 dozers and 600 blast- hole drills. On average, CIL has purchased equipment valued at over $2 billion every year and announced capital expenditure plans worth $6 billion to significantly augment its production capacity in the next five years. This includes plans for setting up 20 new coal preparation plants with a capacity of 111 million MT with estimated capital outlay of $510 million. India's estimated shortfall of thermal coal in 2015 is 189 million MT- 50 percent of the projected demand. Indian power, steel and cement companies are aggressively scouting for coal assets abroad to secure long term coal supply.

Opportunities

CIL is the largest company in India in terms of coal production. The company offers both investment and export opportunities for U.S. companies in the mining sector. It is also actively seeking to buy coal assets abroad, in U.S. and elsewhere. Details of various CIL tenders and investment opportunities, as well as its procurement processes are available in http://www.coalindia.in/ Two other government-owned companies in South India – Singareni Collieries Ltd. in Andhra Pradesh and Neyveli Lignite Corporation in Tamil Nadu -- are other important end users of coal mining equipment. In the private sector, Tata Iron & Steel Company Ltd. (TISCO) in Jamshedpur, Jharkhand continues to be a major buyer of equipment for its captive coal mines. India's private sector power utility companies like Reliance, Adani, RPG Group, Jindal and Tata are also working on projects to develop, own and operate captive coal mines which will require the latest technology and equipment.

The captive mine lessees are under pressure from the government to start mining coal from the virgin coal blocks leased out to them in recent years. These mine owners will resort to mining contractors to start production of coal in the near future.

NMDC Limited is India's largest iron ore producer and exporter, mining about 30 million MT from its three fully mechanized mines. Under expansion plans, the company aims to produce 50 million MT by 2015. It is also in a diversification mode, acquiring new mining leases in iron ore, coal and diamonds. Other large mining companies in India include Essel Mining, Rungta Mines, Orissa Minerals Development Company, Vedanta Resources, Hindalco, Nalco and Steel Authority of India.

Plastics

Overview

Plastics is one of the fastest growing industries in India with a gross turnover of approximately $25 billion and annual growth of 15 percent, making India one of the fastest growing plastic markets in the world. The plastics processing sector is expected to grow significantly as large international companies across industries such as automobile, electronics, telecom, food processing, packaging and healthcare, are setting- up manufacturing facilities in India.

In 2010 U.S. exports of plastic products to India reached $743.8 million. Indian polymers industry is oligopolistic with only three large producers - Reliance Industries Ltd., Haldia Petrochemcial Ltd. and Gas Authority of India Ltd. Major polymers produced in India are polythene (PE), polypropylene (PP) and polyvinyl chloride (PVC). With Reliance commencing operation in Jamnagar, Gujarat for PP and, Indian Oil Corporation (IOC) commissioning a plant in Panipat, Haryana for PP and PEs, it is expected that the demand/supply situation will be balanced for polyethylenes and there will be surplus of PP in coming years. However, the capacity is still expected to be short for polyvinyl chloride and such deficit is likely to continue for several years.

A joint venture between state-owned Hindustan Petroleum Corporation Limited (HPCL) and L N Mittal Group will commence operations soon at a refinery of 9 MMTPA (Million Metric Tonnes per Annum) in Bathinda, Punjab producing clean fuels and polypropylene by processing heavy, sour and acidic crudes. West Bengal Industrial Development Corporation Limited, a Government of West Bengal undertaking, has launched a fully integrated industrial park for petrochemical down-stream industries. Another poly park cluster project is under development at port town of Haldia, 125 km from Kolkata. This park would serve downstream units of Haldia Petrochemicals Limited.. Companies supplying raw materials/equipment in India includes Rohm and Haas, Connell Brothers, GE Silicon, Moserbaer, Honeywell, and Ferromatik Milacorn.

Market Data

Consumption of polymers- plastics, polyethylene, polypropylene and polyvinyl chloride - in terms of total volume of major end products in petrochemicals, increased from 61 percent to 69 percent between 2005 and 2010. Polymers consitute 70 percent of end products of petrochemicals industry in India. Commodity polymers (Polyolefin, PVC, and PS) constitute 85 percent of the market, and Polypropylene and Polyethylene account for 61 percent market share. Indian plastic industry comprises of 23,000+ plastic processing units, 97,000+ processing machines, 23.7 MMT installed processing capacity with an employment of in excess of 3 million people. Additional, 40,800 plastic processing machines are expected to be installed by 2014-2015.

Sub-Sector Best Prospects

Investment opportunities in plastics manufacturing and equipment supplies of $10 billion will exist through year 2020 with installation of 42,000 new machines. In addition, the existing plastic processing capacities offer a significant potential for upgradation through introduction of innovative technologies. Some of the areas with best investment prospects in the plastic industry are:

World-class high capacity machines;

Enhanced design capabilities, moulds, tolls and dies and technological know-how manufacturing and maangement practices with an eye for quality and design;

Development of new products and applications;

Technology consultancy and technology transfer; and

Foreign Direct Investment (FDI) in the downstream sector (including in special economic zones (SEZ), which have beneficial tax regimes).

With the lowest per capita consumption in the world, India is the highest recycler of plastic. Hence there is a huge growth prospect in recycling technology for plastics such as PET bottle recycling, recycling of automotive parts and reuse as blends with virgin material, recycling of e-waste, recycling route for plastic waste to fuel, energy recovery route from plastic waste (incineration), and use of PE & PP waste for road construction (concept of bitumen modifciation by polymer). The estimated investment in local plant and machinery for recycling industries is about $27 million.

Opportunities

India's plastics industry needs the following technologies: multilayer blown film line up to 9/11 layers, automatic block bottom bags production line, high output non-woven machinery, high production and automatic BM machines, higher tonnage injection moulding machines >2000T, stretch blow moulding machines, speciality film and sheet – BOPP/ Cast PP/Multilayer sheet lines and higher tonnage >500 T all electric IM machines. Buyers of plastic technology and equipment in India include A.G. Industries (Automotive), Xpro India Ltd (Films), Jain Irrigation, Supreme Plastics Ltd. , Essel Propack, UFlex Ltd., Machino Plastics Ltd., and Machino Polymers. The U.S. plastic companies in order to enter Indian market may wich to identifiy local partners, agents or distributors. The local partners are familiar with market potential which can be useful for a U.S. exporter. The U.S. companies interested in indentifying business partners in India can use various fee-based services offered by the U.S. Commercial Service office in India.

Power Generation and Clean and Renewable Energy

Overview

India has the fifth largest generation capacity in the world with an installed capacity of 182,344 MW which is about 4 percent of global power generation. Both government and private sector firms generate electric power in India, with the government sector leading the pack. National Hydroelectric Power Corporation, National Thermal Power Corporation and various state level corporations (State Electricity Boards - SEBs) are the major players. SEBs or private companies oversee the transmission and distribution (T&D).

The existing electric power supply is still 30 percent less than the demand. Annual per capita consumption of electricity in India in FY 2010 was approx. 779 KW, which is less than 5 percent of

U.S. per capita consumption. There has been significant improvement in the growth in actual generation - 61,595 MW of the new generation was added during the last five years. Out of the total installed capacity, private sector companies produce about 21 percent (as of March 2011). The rest is produced by the central government and various state governments. India needs 270,000 MW of installed capacity to be able to meet its peak electricity demand. The Government of India (GOI) had set ambitious goals of capacity addition of 75,785 MW by 2017 of which 50 percent will be added by private sector. India aims to achieve capacity growth rate of 9 percent per annum. Approximately 80 percent of the incremental capacity is expected to be thermal.

However, coal availability to meet this demand is uncertain, and therefore significant emphasis is expected on alternate sources like renewable and nuclear power. The Integrated Energy Policy promulgated by the GOI has estimated energy requirements in the year 2030 to be about 950,000 MW. According to the Indian Prime Minster, Dr. Manmohan Singh, the government will help and promote Public - Private Partnerships (PPP) to meet the estimated $1.2 trillion investment required over the next 25 years to provide electricity to consumers at an affordable cost. The private sector opportunity in energy infrastructure during the next 5 years is estimated at US$195 billion dollars. Demand for investment across the power industry will generate opportunities for various participants in the value chain including equipment manufacturers and service providers.

There will be strong demand for power equipment; construction and material handling equipment; transport equipment, EPC contracting, electronic and IT systems, environmental technologies; financial services, education and training, design and planning services and advisory and professional services. The United States continues to be one of the largest exporters of generation and transmission equipment to India along with China, Germany, Japan and the U.K.

Opportunities

Transmission and Distribution: The source of the power sector's ailments is the poor operational efficiency of the SEBs. Due to subsidized tariffs to residential and agricultural consumers, low investment in transmission and distribution (T&D) systems, inadequate maintenance, and high levels of distribution losses (which is about 33 percent in India), theft, and uncollected bills, the SEBs are continually in financial distress. The current installed transmission capacity is only 13 percent of the total installed generated capacity. With a focus on increasing generation capacity over the next 5 years, the corresponding investments in the transmission sector is also expected to increase. While 100 percent foreign direct investment (FDI) is allowed in the power sector, so far the existing private sector participation is primarily from domestic players but there has been emerging interest from foreign players in the sector: AES and China Light and Power have been in India for the last 10 years, but there is increasing interest from new European and Asian players.

Private sector participation in distribution is increasing as the public sector Power Grid Corporation has not been able to generate sufficient investments. The GOI is now actively encouraging private sector participation in transmission through PPPs and has identified select projects for implementation through competitive bidding. Opportunities in transmission capacity addition exist in the development of the National Grid and intra-state transmission lines, Ultra Mega transmission projects (of 16000 MW), and transmission joint venture projects. Seven inter-state transmission projects have been awarded to private sector. In addition, global tendering processes for five additional projects with an aggregate capital expenditure of $1.2 billion are in various stages of award.

Encouraged by the success of the GOI, several state governments have also identified intra-state transmission lines for implementation under the PPP framework through the franchise route and 3 such projects have been awarded recently. There are distribution franchise opportunities in Maharashtra, Madhya Pradesh, and several other states. India is seeking to diversify and grow its energy sources and reduce carbon emissions in the context of sustained economic expansion. With the rapid growth of the Indian economy, the demand for clean technologies in the country is rising exponentially, and the development of renewable energy resources and deployment of environment technologies that reduce greenhouse gas emissions is a high priority for the Government of India.

Renewable Energy: The Indian renewable energy market is estimated to be worth over $17 billion this year and is growing at an annual rate of 15 percent. Wind, hydro, solar, biomass, and waste-to-energy all have huge potential. Only 19,973 MW of total renewable energy potential estimated at 200,000 MW has been tapped in India thus far leaving a huge opportunity for potential future market growth. India today stands among the top four countries in the world in terms of renewable energy capacity and it offers some attractive incentives in this area.

Wind: India plans to increase fifty percent share of capacity addition in renewable energy by 2017. Approximately 20 billion investments expected during 2012-17. U.S. companies can take advantage of India's wind energy market, which is one of the world's largest as India imports wind turbines, windmill blades, wind battery chargers, wind energy converters etc. Hydro: The hydropower generation potential for India is 300,000 MW out of which only 145,000 MW can be exploited due to limited resources and difficult geographical terrain. The GOI has firmed up an investment of $20 billion for the development of hydro projects by 2020. Biomass: The GOI announced a target of creating 10,000 MW of biomass power generation by 2020 and will shortly release a biomass power policy to chart out a roadmap for supporting biomass generated power.

Waste to Energy: The GOI has developed a National Master Plan for Development of Waste to Energy in India. The GOI estimates that the potential to generate power from municipal solid waste will more than double by 2020, while the potential from industrial waste is likely to increase by more than 50 percent. In a country with high population density and limited landfill capacity, waste to energy power generation is a major priority. Solar: India has embarked upon a $20 billion plan to produce 22GW of solar power by 2022. So far India uses only about 140 MW, which can provide enough power to serve a town of 50,000 people. Developers of solar farms in India have shown preference for thin –film solar cells offered by U.S., Taiwan and European suppliers. Nuclear: opportunities in equipment and technology expected to boost India's nuclear power plants, but the process has slowed because of the environmental and security concerns and continued concerns over potential liability exposure for foreign players.

Energy Efficiency: The market potential for industrial energy efficiency products and services is projected to be approximately $27 billion in 2018. Opportunities in efficiency improvement include smart grid metering and smart grids, IT and operation improvement.

Smart Grids: At present the smart grid market in India is at a nascent stage but is projected to grow rapidly with plans to install several million smart meters in the next few years. Green Buildings: India has emerged as one of the world's top destinations for green buildings and has implemented a number of home-rating schemes and building codes, which open up a wide range of opportunities for U.S. companies in the energy efficiency sector.

Travel and Tourism

Overview

India is one of the fastest growing outbound travel markets in the world. Industry estimates suggest that the current outbound figures stand at 12 million travelers and with double-digit growth in the years to come the market is expected to expand to 50 million travelers by 2020. The growth of the Indian economy has translated into a tremendous upward mobility for Indian consumers now having spending-power like never before. This increasing amount of surplus cash in the hands of both the middle-classes, as well as the higher socio-economic class, has had a direct impact on the Indian outbound travel industry.

An increased standard of living has allowed first-time travelers to realize a long-held dream to travel overseas. With the introduction of new low-cost carriers such as Air Asia in India, the cost of travelling to many outbound destinations has also declined significantly. This has given a further boost to outbound travel, as statistics reveal that many Indians have started opting for value-for-money outbound vacation packages over domestic packages. For the more affluent, travel is moving higher up on their list of priorities. The industry has seen the upper socio-economic classes take more trips abroad, and has noted changing trends and expectations for their vacations. Adventure holidays, sports holidays and luxury vacations are gaining popularity among this segment. In 2011, there were 10,909,000 resident departures from India. This was a 10.19 percent growth over the previous year. Out of this figure, 4,770,000 departures were to the Asia Pacific region; 3,042,000 to the Middle East; 1,576,000 to Europe; and 1,177,000 to Singapore.

It's clear that countries around Asia are the most popular destinations for Indians traveling overseas – accounting for 72 percent of leisure trips and 63 percent of business trips. Europe, like the US attracts a greater percentage of Indian travelers for business, rather than pleasure. In 2010 over 651,000 Indian tourists visited the United States, registering an increase of 139 percent since 2003. According to a projection released recently by The International Trade Administration (ITA), an agency of the U.S. Department of Commerce, the U.S. anticipates a 50 percent increase in the number of travelers from India by 2016. Interestingly, Indian tourists visiting the U.S. in 2010 spent an average of $4,390, totaling to over a staggering $2.86 billion.

A factsheet on India prepared by the ITA said that an overwhelming majority of Indian tourists visit the U.S. either for business / professional reasons or visiting friends and relatives. Only a small percentage of them -- less than 10 percent- visit the U.S. for leisure or vacation. The report also said that for nearly 1/3 of Indian tourists, the U.S. was their first travel overseas. On an average, an Indian tourist visited 1.8 American states and stayed in the U.S. for over a month-and-a-half. Families and couples are likely to be the primary consumer segments of the future. This segment along with the first along with first time travelers will be the key to increased outbound tourism from India into the United States. The key travel motivation of potential first-time visitors to the US is a cultural/sightseeing vacation.

Travel motivation among repeat visitors is a cultural/sightseeing vacation, touring/driving holiday. Now countries and destinations worldwide are seeking a share of this ever-expanding Indian outbound market. It is imperative of for the US travel industry to increase its visibility in this market to get a share of the Indian outbound tourist who today has travel options like never before.

Sub-Sector Best Prospects

MICE (Meeting, Incentives, Conference and Exhibitions),

Honeymoon

Luxury

Adventure tours

Escorted group tours

Opportunities

The ever-increasing amounts of how much Indians spend overseas prove that not only are Indians determined to travel more, they are also determined to spend more, every year. Besides global branded goods, accessories, electronics, local souvenirs, fine gifts, fragrances and fashion, Indians are increasingly splurging on travel and accommodation. The travel trend has also been changing. While business travel, holiday and VFR (Visiting Family and Friends) trips still dominate outbound volumes, there is a new trend of people opting for niche products like sports tourism, luxury travels, honeymoon packages and cruises. It is not uncommon for affluent Indians today to plan trips around cricket matches, golf tournaments, tennis matches, Formula-1 races, etc.

Another fast-growing segment for outbound travel from India is MICE (Meeting, Incentives, Conference and Exhibitions) group-travel. Companies in India are realizing the benefits that accrue to their businesses from organizing MICE trips, which involve large or small groups of people from their company or industry meeting at interesting foreign destinations for conferences, trade exhibitions, focused business meetings, or just recreation. Tour operators have been staying on top of their game by offering new value-added services, like discounted tickets for sports tournaments, shopping deals and discounts at destination countries, special honeymoon packages, MICE packages, etc.

Chapter 5: Leading Agricultural Sectors for U.S. Export and Investment

Agriculture's share in India's overall GDP is gradually declining with the current share at less than 14 percent while nearly 60 percent of the population depends on agriculture for their livelihood. Overall economic growth would be improved by a better performing agricultural sector, which is why growth in the sector is a priority of the Indian government. The government maintains a costly price support system for wheat and rice, and also subsidizes fertilizer, credit and other farm inputs. State governments provide farmers with free or subsidized electricity and irrigation water. The cumulative effect of these interventions has been to distort prices, planting patterns, and marketing.

The agriculture sector suffers from declining public, and relatively small private, investment. There is a shortage of warehouses and cold storage facilities, causing losses due to spoilage. Infrastructure such as roads, telecommunications, and electricity are inadequate in rural areas and impede agricultural growth. Although the 'organized' retailing is growing with several large Indian corporations entering and expanding their operations, the recent economic slowdown had a temporary negative impact on this sector. The optimism in the food retail sector stems from a vibrant and growing economy, increasing purchasing power, and an increasing number of urban consumers demanding a more international shopping experience. This provides an opportunity for the supply of various U.S. food products to India. However, success in introducing a new product in this highly price sensitive market depends on an effective pricing strategy and familiarity with India's myriad food laws. High import tariffs and competition from inexpensive domestic and third country products are other challenges.

Cotton

India is the world's second largest producer and exporter of cotton. India will be in the export market for the next few years, until domestic consumption catches up with the production surge. However, India will continue to import extra long staple (ELS) and quality long staple cotton (28-34 mm), with occasional imports of medium staple cotton when international prices are favorable. The United States has been the leading supplier of cotton to India over the past few years. U.S. cotton exports to India in CY 2011 were valued at about $ 93.1 million. Other major suppliers include Egypt, Commonwealth of Independent States (CIS), and West Africa. Indian mills that import US Pima and upland cotton are appreciative of its superior quality, consistency and higher ginning yield.

Tree Nuts and Dry Fruits

Dry fruits and nuts (primarily almonds), have been one of the leading U.S. agricultural exports to India in the past, with exports in CY 2011 estimated at a record $308.2 million. The United States is the largest supplier of almonds (mostly in-shell) to India, with a market share of about 85 percent. Other suppliers include Australia, Syria, China, Iran, and Afghanistan. Afghani almonds enjoy a 100 percent concession on the basic import duty under the Indo-Afghan trade agreement. Almonds are a preferred nut in India and are gaining popularity among the growing middle-income population due to their nutritional and health benefits. India also imports small quantities of dates, pistachios, hazel nuts, prunes, and raisins, mainly from the United States, Iran, Afghanistan, Pakistan, and the Middle East.

Wood Products
India has removed virtually all non-tariff trade barriers on wood product imports, although tariffs remain high. The domestic market is highly price sensitive and scarce supplies and high prices have limited the use of wood in construction and other sectors. Dwindling domestic supplies and restrictions on tree felling due to environmental concerns are likely to result in a more liberal import regime over the coming years. U.S. wood and wood products exports to India in CY 2011 were valued at a record $31 million.

Fresh Fruits
India provides market access for most fresh fruits, although tariffs are high. With a growing segment of consumers insisting on high standards and year-round availability, there is an increasing demand for imported fresh fruits. U.S. exports of fresh fruit (mostly apples and table grapes) to India in CY 2011 were valued at $ 101 million. Market sources expect imports to continue to show excellent growth over the coming years, with new products expected to enter the Indian market.

Pulses

India is the world's largest importer of pulses (peas, lentils, and beans), with annual imports ranging from 2.5-3.8 million tons. In IFY 2010/11 (Apr-Mar) imports totaled 2.8 million tons. India is primarily a price (rather than quality) market with imports sourced largely from Canada, Myanmar, Australia, and France. The typically higher priced U.S. green and yellow peas and lentils have become more price competitive in the Indian market in recent years due to domestic shortages and higher prices. As a result, imports of pulses from the U.S., (mostly dry green peas and some yellow peas), witnessed significant growth during the past 5 years, reaching a record 224 thousand tons in CY 2009. While U.S. pulse exports declined to 98,700 tons in CY 2011, India is still one of the leading markets for U.S. pulses. Pulses are currently exempted from import tariffs.

Vegetable Oil

India is the world's second largest edible oil importer after the EU-27, with 2011-12(Oct-Sep) imports estimated at 9.1 million tons. While lower priced palm oil has traditionally dominated this price-sensitive market, exporters with competitively priced supplies of other oils, (for example soybean, cottonseed, corn, or sunflower oil), often find buyers in India. Food inflation concerns prompted the Indian government to eliminate the import duty on most crude edible vegetable oils and to lower the import duty on refined vegetable oils to 7.5 percent. In CY 2010, U.S. soybean oil was price competitive in India, resulting in commercial sales of around $133 million dollar, up 11 percent over CY 2009. CY 2011 exports were negligible due to higher U.S. prices.

Planting Seeds

Indian imports of planting seeds, mostly for vegetables and flowers in Indian fiscal year 2010/11 (April/March) were valued at $63.6 million, with a U.S. share of over $6 million. The Indian seed industry is undergoing a transformation, which includes an increasing role for private seed companies, the rising presence of multinational seed companies, and wide-ranging changes in the regulatory framework. All of these will likely affect seed research, marketing, and trade in coming years. With demand for high quality fruits and vegetables growing from domestic consumers and the food processing industry, India's seed imports are likely to grow. Snack Foods Consumers' changing life styles and the increasing disposable income of the middle class have spurred rising demand for imported snack foods, despite competition from local players. CY 2011exports of U.S. snack foods to India reached a record $7 million.

Hides and Skins

India imported hides and skins worth $92.16 million during Indian CY 2010, about 20 percent over the previous year. (Complete CY 2011 data is not yet available). These were primarily used by the booming leather goods export sector. While India has historically imported from Europe, exporters from New Zealand, Myanmar, the Middle East and Africa have emerged as significant competitors. Imports of hides and skins from U.S. suppliers fell from approximately 3 million dollars in 2010 to 750 thousand dollars in 2011 (75 percent). Raw hide imports attract a zero tariff in India while wet blues attract a tariff of 14.71 percent.

Chapter 6: Trade Regulations, Customs and Standards

Import Tariffs

In 1991, India began to initiate economic reforms that have made the trade regime increasingly more transparent. These reforms are complimented by a consistent decline in import tariff rates over the past 15 years – from peak rates of 350 percent in June 1991 to an average of 10 percent today. However, India's tariffs are still relatively high by international standards, and these high tariffs and import restrictions have constrained U.S. firms from selling in this market, and U.S. investors from importing competitive inputs in several industries. India's current regulations are guided by the Export Import (EXIM) Policy of 2009-2014. Imports are permitted in most cases without a license. There are some exceptions where items are prohibited or restricted (import permitted under license) or where imports are allowed only through a state-owned enterprise.

As of April 2001, India removed quantitative restrictions (QR) on a final batch of 715 items, completing the process of phased trade policy liberalization that was started in 1991. India has appealed to the Appellate Body of the World Trade Organization against the recommendations of a WTO panel report on its quantitative restrictions on the import of agricultural, textile, and industrial products. India has challenged the panel's authority to determine whether the balance of payments can be used to justify imposition of import restrictions and the overall compatibility of regional trade agreements with WTO norms. The removal of

QRs and the prospect of further reduction in tariffs to the Asian levels are likely to lead to a high degree of import competition.

Tariff Rates: India has progressively cut duties and taxes since 1991, after it began switching from a Socialist-style system to a market economy. However, domestic industry still enjoys relatively high levels of protection in several areas. U.S. companies face tariff and non-tariff barriers that impede their exports. One such area of protection is in the agricultural sector where Indian tariffs remain high compared to international standards. For non-agricultural goods, however, India has made considerable progress in restructuring tariffs. In February 2007, the Government of India (GOI) further reduced the peak applied customs duty on non-agricultural goods from 12.5 percent to 10 percent. The Indian government plans to gradually ease currency restrictions and reduce tariffs to the low levels prevailing in other Asian countries in order to make the Indian environment more conducive to improved economic performance.

Classification: As there are thousands of goods that are imported into India, it is not possible to prescribe rates of duty for each type of merchandise. The basic applicable legislation is the Indian Customs Act of 1962, and the Customs Tariff Act of 1975. The Customs Act of 1962 was created to control imports and prevent Illegal imports and exports of goods. The Customs Tariff Act specifies the tariffs rates and provides for the imposition of anti-dumping and countervailing duties. The Indian customs classification on tariff items follows the Harmonized Commodity Description and Coding System (Harmonized System or HS). Customs uses six-digit HS codes, the Directorate-General of

Commercial Intelligence and Statistics (DGCI&S) uses eight-digit codes for statistical purposes, and the Directorate General of Foreign Trade (DGFT) has broadly extended the eight-digit DGCI&S codes up to 10 digits. It is also worth noting that the excise authorities use HS codes for classifying goods to levy excise duty (manufacturing taxes) on goods produced in India. All goods imported into India are subject to duty. There are several factors that go into calculating customs duty, including:

Basic Customs Duty (BCD): This duty is levied either as 1) a specific rate based on the unit of the item (weight, number, etc.), or more commonly, 2) ad-valorem, based on the assessable value of the item. In some cases, a combination of the two is used.

Additional Customs Duty (ACD): This duty is typically referred to as Countervailing duty or (CVD) and is levied on the assessed value of goods plus basic customs duty. Goods that fall into this category are imported goods that have similar goods manufactured in India. The objective is to protect domestic industry from imports.

Special Additional Customs Duty (known as Special CVD): Earlier known as surcharge, Special CVD tax is applicable on all items. It is levied at the rate of 4 percent of the basic and the excise duty on all imports.

Anti-dumping Duty: This is levied on specified goods imported from specified countries, including the United States, to protect indigenous industry from injury. *Safeguard Duty*: The Indian government may by notification impose a safeguard duty on articles after concluding that increased imported quantities and under current conditions will cause or threaten to cause serious injury to domestic industry.

Customs Education Cess: Effective July 2004, India introduced a new education cess (duty) assessment. The current rate is three percent of Basic Customs Duty (BCD) and Additional Duty of Customs (ACD). Goods bound under international commitments have been exempted from this cess. Customs Handling Fee: The Indian government assesses a one percent customs handling fee on all imports in addition to the applied customs duty. Total Duty: Therefore, for most goods, total duty payable = BCD + ACD + Special CVD + Education Cess + Customs Handling Fee. Tariff rates, excise duties, regulatory duties, and countervailing duties are revised in each annual budget in February, and are published in various sources, including BIGs Easy Reference Customs Tariff edition. A copy of this book is kept at the USA Trade Information Center in Washington DC and more specific information from this guide is available to U.S. Companies by calling 800-USA-TRADE. While the Indian government publishes customs tariffs rates there is no single official publication that has all information on tariffs and tax rates on imports. Moreover, each Indian State levies taxes on interstate trade and commerce, which adds to the confusion. Effective April 2005, the Indian government implemented a Value-Added tax (VAT) system meant to replace the inter-state taxes, but implementation is not yet universal in all the States.

Duty exemption plan: The Duty Exemption Plan enables duty free import of inputs required for export production. An advance license is issued under the duty exemption plan. The Duty Remission Plan enables post export replenishment remission of duty on inputs used in the export product. Duty Remission plan consists of (a) DFRC and (b) DEPB. DFRC permits duty free import charges on inputs used in the export product. The government has wide discretionary power to declare full or partial duty exemptions "in the public interest" and to specify conditions such as end-use provisions. Almost half of India's total inputs enter under concessional tariffs, though the use of exemptions is falling in tandem with the tariff-reduction program.

Trade Barriers

Any restriction imposed on the free flow of trade is a trade barrier. Trade barriers can either be tariff barriers (the levy of ordinary negotiated customs duties in accordance with Article II of the GATT) or non-tariff barriers, which are any trade barriers other than tariff barriers. Import Licensing: One of the most common non-tariff barriers is the prohibition or restrictions on imports maintained through import licensing requirements. Though India has eliminated its import licensing requirements for most consumer goods, certain products face licensing related trade barriers. For example, the Indian government requires a special import license for motorcycles and vehicles that is very restrictive. Import licenses for motorcycles are provided to only foreign nationals permanently residing in India, working in India for foreign firms that hold greater than 30 percent equity or to foreign nations working at embassies and foreign missions. Some domestic importers are allowed to import vehicles without a license provided the imports are counterbalanced by exports attributable to the same importer.

Standards, testing, labeling & certification: The Indian government has identified 109 commodities that must be certified by its National Standards body, the Bureau of Indian Standards (BIS). The idea behind these certifications is to ensure the quality of goods seeking access into the market, but many countries use them as protectionist measures.

Anti-dumping and countervailing measures: Anti-dumping and countervailing measures are permitted by the WTO Agreements in specified situations to protect the domestic industry from serious injury arising from dumped or subsidized imports. India imposes these from time-to-time to protect domestic manufacturers from dumping. India's implementation of its antidumping policy has, in some cases, raised concerns regarding transparency and due process. In recent years, India seems to have aggressively increased its application of the antidumping law. Export subsidies and domestic support: Several export subsidies and other domestic support is provided to several industries to make them competitive internationally. Export earnings are exempt from taxes and exporters are not subject to local manufacturing tax. While export subsidies tend to displace exports from other countries into third country markets, the domestic support acts as a direct barrier against access to the domestic market.

Procurement: The Indian government allows a price preference for local suppliers in government contracts and generally discriminates against foreign suppliers. In international purchases and International Competitive Bids (ICB's) domestic companies gets a price preference in government contract and purchases.

Service barriers: Services in which there are restrictions include: insurance, banking, securities, motion pictures, accounting, construction, architecture and engineering, retailing, legal services, express delivery services and telecommunication.

Other barriers: Equity restrictions and other trade-related investment measures are in place to give an unfair advantage to domestic companies. The GOI continues to limit or prohibit FDI in sensitive sectors such as retail trade and agriculture. Additionally there is an unpublished policy that favors counter trade. Several Indian companies, both government-owned and private, conduct a small amount of counter trade.

Import Requirements and Documentation

Import licensing requirements: In the last decade, India has steadily replaced licensing and discretionary controls over imports with deregulation and simpler import procedures. The majority of import items fall within the scope of India's EXIM Policy regulation of Open General License (OGL). This means that they are deemed to be freely importable without restrictions and without a license, except to the extent that they are regulated by the provisions of the Policy or any other law. Imports of items not covered by OGL are regulated, and fall into three categories: banned or prohibited items, restricted items requiring an import license, and "canalized" items importable only by government trading monopolies and subject to Cabinet approval regarding timing and quantity.

The following are designated import certificate issuing authorities:

The Department of Electronics for import of computer and computer related systems

The Department of Industrial Policy and Promotion for organized sector firms except for import of computers and computer based systems

The Ministry of Defense for defense related items

The Director General of Foreign Trade for small-scale industries not covered in the foregoing.

Capital goods can be imported with a license under the Export Promotion Capital Goods plan (EPCG) at reduced rates of duty, subject to the fulfillment of a time-bound export obligation. The EPGC plan now applies to all industry sectors. It is also applicable to all capital goods without any threshold limits, on payment of a 5 percent customs duty. A duty exemption plan is also offered under which imports of raw materials, intermediates, components, consumables, parts, accessories and packing materials required for direct use in products to be exported may be permitted free of duty under various categories of licenses. For the actual user, a non-transferable advance license is one such license. For those who do not wish to go through the advance-licensing route, a post-export duty-free replenishment certificate is available.

Advance License: An advance license is issued to allow duty free import of inputs, which are physically incorporated in the export product (making normal allowance for wastage). In addition, fuel, oil, energy, catalysts etc. that are consumed in the course of their use to obtain the export product, may also be allowed under the plan. Duty free import of mandatory spares up to 10 percent of the CIF value of the license, which are required to be exported/ supplied with the resultant product, may also be allowed under Advance License.

Advance license can be issued for:

Physical exports: An advance license may be issued for physical exports to a manufacturer exporter or merchant exporter tied to supporting manufacturer(s) for import of inputs required for the export product.

Intermediate supplies: An advance license may be issued for intermediate supply to a manufacturer- exporter for the import of inputs required in the manufacture of goods to be supplied to the ultimate exporter/deemed exporter holding another Advance License.

Deemed exports: An advance license can be issued for deemed exports to the main contractor for import of inputs required in the manufacture of goods. An advance license for deemed exports can also be availed by the sub-contractor of the main contractor to such project provided the name of the sub contractor(s) appears in the main contract. Such license for deemed export can also be issued for supplies made to United Nations Organizations or under the Aid Program of the United Nations or other multilateral agencies and paid for in foreign exchange.

Import Declaration: Importers are required to furnish an import declaration in the prescribed bill of entry format, disclosing full details of the value of imported goods. Import Licenses (if applicable): All import documents must be accompanied by any import licenses. This will enable the customs to clear the documents and allow the import without delay. Ex-factory invoice, freight and insurance certificates: These must be attached so that the customs can verify the price and decide on the classification under which the import tariff can be calculated.

Letter of Credit (L/C): All importers must accompany a copy of the L/C to ensure that payment for the import is made. Normally this document is counter-checked with the issuing bank so that outflow of foreign exchange is checked. Not all consignments are inspected prior to clearance, and inspection may be dispensed with for reputable importers. In the current customs set-up, an appointment with the clearing agents for clearance purposes will avoid delays. In general, documentation requirements, including ex-factory bills of sale, are extensive and delays are frequent.

These cost investors time and money, including additional detention and demurrage charges, making it more expensive to operate and invest in India. For delayed clearances, importers seek release of shipments against a performance bond; furnishing a bank guarantee for this purpose is a more expensive proposition. Customs have recently extended operations to 24 hours a day to ensure timely clearance of export cargo.

U.S. Export Controls

The Indian and the U.S. governments formed a High Technology Cooperation Group (HTCG) in November 2002 to facilitate and promote high technology bilateral trade. The Bureau of Industry and Security (BIS) (formerly known as the Bureau of Export Administration, BXA) is the American government agency responsible for implementing and enforcing the Export Administration Regulations (EAR), which regulate the export and re-export of most commercial items. The BIS often refers to the items that they regulate as "dual- use" items, since these items have both commercial and military or proliferation applications, but purely commercial items without an obvious military use are also subject to the EAR.

Temporary Entry

The Indian Customs Act, 1962 allows import of goods on a temporary basis into India. Section 74 of the Act provides for drawback on goods that are imported for a temporary period into India and exported out of the country. As per the Section 74, drawback is allowable on re-export of duty paid goods. When the goods are re- exported out of India, the exporter will be entitled to a drawback of a specified percentage of the duty paid at the time of import.

The procedure for claiming duty drawback under Section 74 is governed by provisions of the Re-Export of Imported Goods (Drawback of Customs Duties) Rules, 1995. The rate of drawback available depends upon the time period for which the goods are stored in India or put to use. If goods are re-exported without being put to use in India, 98 percent of the customs duty would be available as duty drawback, provided that the exports have taken place within 24 months from the date of import. However, under section 75 of the Act, where the goods are used in India subsequent to their import, the drawback is determined on the basis of the duration of use of the goods in India (the length of period from the date of clearance for home consumption and the date goods are placed under customs control for export). The procedure for claiming duty drawback under Section 75 is governed by provisions of the Customs and Central Excise Duties Drawback Rules 1995. In addition, General Exemption No 14 of the Customs Tariff allows the import of goods for display or use at fair, exhibition, demonstration, seminar, congress and conferences, subject to specified conditions.

ATA Carnet: An ATA Carnet is an International Uniform Customs document issued in 71 countries including India, which are parties to the Customs Convention on ATA Carnet. The ATA Carnet permits duty free temporary admission of goods into a member country without the need to raise customs bond, payment of duty and fulfillment of other customs formalities in one or a number of foreign countries. The initials "ATA" are an acronym of the French and English word "Admission Temporaire / Temporary Admission". Within the ICC World Chambers Federation, the World ATA Carnet Council (WATAC) runs the ATA system and its international guarantee chain. The Council is made up of representatives from the countries and territories where Carnets are issued and accepted. Each country in the system has a single guaranteeing body approved by the national customs authorities and the ICC World Chambers

Federation (Until June 2001, the International Bureau of Chambers of Commerce). The WCF is sponsored by the International Chamber of Commerce (ICC) in Paris. In India, Federation of Indian Chambers of Commerce and Industry (FICCI), is appointed as National Guaranteeing & Issuing Association for ATA Carnets.

Labeling and Marking Requirements

Labeling is an important element for products being exported to India. English is the favorable language for labeling. All packets or even containers should carry information depending upon the consignment. Indian Customs are strict and ensure that imported items have the legally required information before these enter the retail market or are sold for consumption, excluding those products that fall under the EOU segment. As per a Notification issued by the Ministry of Commerce on November 24, 2000, all pre-packaged commodities (intended for direct retail sale only) imported into India must carry the following declarations on the label:

Name and address of the importer.

Generic or common name of the commodity packed.

Net quantity in terms of standard unit of weights and measurement.

All units of weight or measurements must be metric. If the net quantity of the imported package is given in any other unit, its equivalent of standard units must be declared by the importer.

Month and year of packing in which the commodity is manufactured, packed or imported, and

The maximum retail sales price (MRP) at which the commodity in packaged form may be sold to the end consumer. The MRP includes all taxes, freight transport charges, commission payable to dealers, and all charges towards advertising, delivery, packing, forwarding and the like.

Compliance of the above-stated requirements has to be ensured before the import consignments are cleared by Customs in India. The import of pre-packaged commodities such as raw materials, components, bulk import etc., that need to undergo further processing before they are sold to end consumers are not included under this labeling requirement.

Standards

Overview

Standards setting as a trend is gaining momentum in India. India has generally made efforts to match] national standards in line with international norms, and most Indian standards are harmonized with ISO standards. Nonetheless, some Indian standards are not matched with international standards, and several recent standards-related regulations have created barriers to trade and posed challenges to expanding U.S. exports in certain sectors. India has also frequently failed to notify the WTO of new standards and allow time for discussion with its trading partners prior to implementation.

Because of pressure from consumer rights groups, NGOs, and environmental activists there is a growing emphasis on product standards in India in various industry sectors. The proactive role of the judiciary in formulating legal framework and regulations for better standards and control in sectors such as the environment have also contributed to an increased awareness and emphasis on product standards in India. But, for instance, while Indian food safety laws are outdated or in some cases more stringent than international norms, enforcement is weak.

Standards Organizations

In India, voluntary standards are exclusively developed by the national standards body. The Bureau of Indian Standards (BIS), established under the Bureau of Indian Standards Act of 1986, is the national standards body of India responsible for development and formulation of standards. BIS is comprised of representatives of industry, consumer organizations, scientific and research bodies, professional organizations, technical institutions, Indian government ministries, and members of parliament. Besides development and formulation of Indian Standards, BIS is involved with product certification, quality system certifications and testing, and consumer affairs.

The Ministry of Commerce, Government of India (GOI) has designated BIS as the National WTO-TBT Enquiry Point in accordance with its obligations to the agreement on Technical Barriers to Trade of the WTO. According to the agreement, BIS in liaison with the Indian Ministry of Commerce, issues notifications on proposed technical regulations and certification systems in India to the WTO. BIS's Technical Information Services Center responds to domestic and foreign requests for information about Indian standards, technical regulations and conformity assessment rules. U.S. companies that wish to make comments on any notifications can obtain copies of the text from BIS from the WTO-TBT Enquiry Point, Technical Information Services Center in BIS. BIS communicates comments to the Ministry of Commerce. BIS is the only organization in India authorized to operate quality certification plans under an Act of Parliament. It serves as the official member and sets policy for Indian participation in the International Organization for Standardization (ISO) and International Electro technical Commission (IEC). NIST Notify U.S. Service Member countries of the World Trade Organization (WTO) are required under the Agreement on Technical Barriers to Trade (TBT Agreement) to report to the WTO all proposed technical regulations that could affect trade with other Member countries.

Product Certification

BIS's product standards are basically voluntary in nature, but subsequent to the removal of quantitative restrictions (QRs) on imports by India in 2000, the GOI, in order to provide protection to domestic producers in certain sectors, promulgated regulations dictating that imports of 109 products are subject to mandatory compliance with specified Indian quality standards. For compliance, all exporters/manufacturers of the 109 products are required to register with, and obtain certification from the Bureau of Indian Standards, before exporting such goods to India. The list of 109 products includes various food preservatives and additives, milk powder, infant milk food, certain kinds of cement, household and similar electrical appliances, several types of gas cylinders, and multi-purpose dry batteries.

These 109 products generally must be tested and certified by BIS in India. BIS now however, also has a system for foreign companies to receive automatic certification for products not manufactured in India. The system is based on a self-certification basis, under which a foreign manufacturer is permitted to apply the standards mark on the product after ascertaining its conformity to the Indian Standard licensed for. At the foreign manufacturer's expense, BIS inspectors travel to the manufacturer's country to inspect their production facility to pre-certify the company and its production system, and then authorizes subsequent monitoring and compliance by an independent inspector to ensure that the company maintains the specified standards.

Information on the application procedure for BIS Product Certification Plan for foreign companies is available through the BIS website. Exporters/manufacturers of these products also are required to maintain a presence in India. This requirement does not apply if the foreign manufacturer nominates an authorized representative in India who agrees to be responsible for compliance with the provisions of BIS on behalf of the foreign manufacturer as per an agreement signed between the manufacturer and BIS. Under separate arrangements some products have been placed under special certification plans of lot or batch inspections carried out by BIS inspecting officers.

A majority of gas cylinders, deep well hand pumps and valves are certified through such plans. To facilitate international trade and cooperation, India has plans to harmonize its standards with other countries, primarily with its main trading partners. A serious effort is being made by BIS to have mutual recognition of standards with various countries so that other countries provide recognition of the Indian standards on certain products and vice versa. The BIS has expressed interest in having mutual recognition agreements with U.S. organizations.

Accreditation

The National Accreditation Board for Testing and Calibration Laboratories (NABL) established in 1985 as an autonomous body under the Department of Science & Technology is authorized by the GOI as the sole accreditation body for testing and calibration laboratories. More than 200 testing and calibration laboratories have been accredited to date. For international mutual acceptance of test results in order to be compliant with the WTO/Technical Barriers to Trade (TBT) regulations, NABL is a member of international organizations such as International Laboratory Accreditation Co-operation (ILAC) and Asia Pacific Laboratory Accreditation Co-operation (APLAC). NABL is a signatory to ILAC as well as APLAC Mutual Recognition Arrangements (MRA), based on mutual evaluation and acceptance of other MRA Partner laboratory accreditation systems.

More and more Indian manufacturing companies are investing in standards accreditation. The number of plants in India with ISO 9000 and ISO 14000 accreditation increased from a negligible figure in the early nineties to more than 8000 in 2003. Five Indian companies have won the Deming prize for total quality management in FY 2002-03, while eight more are preparing for the honours this year. Eighteen manufacturing plants of 10

Indian companies have been recognised by the Japanese Institute of Plant Management for excelling in total productive management in 2003.

Trade Agreements

India has entered into bilateral and regional trading agreements over the years. These agreements, besides offering preferential tariff rates on the trade of goods among member countries, also provide for wider economic cooperation in the fields of trade in services, investment, and intellectual property. The preferential arrangement/plans under which India is receiving tariff preferences are the Generalized System of Preferences (GSP) and the Global System of Trade Preferences (GSTP). Presently, there are 46 member countries of the GSTP and India has exchanged tariff concessions with 12 countries on a limited number of products.

Other such preferential arrangements include the South Asian Association for Regional Cooperation (SAARC) Preferential Trading Agreement (SAPTA), the Bangkok Agreement and India–Sri Lanka Free Trade Agreement (ISLFTA). These arrangements/ agreements prescribe Rules of Origin that have to be fulfilled for exports to be eligible for tariff preference. India and several Asian countries have signed a Comprehensive Economic Cooperation Agreement (CECA), which is an integrated package of agreements embracing trade in goods, services, investments and economic co-operations in education, science and technology, air services, and intellectual property.

The agreements provide wide-ranging exemptions and reductions on basic customs duty on products imported from Singapore into India.

The Indian Ministry of Commerce projected that 60 percent of India's future trade would be accounted for by free trade agreements (FTAs), with such countries as Paraguay, Argentina, Brazil, Pakistan and even China. In a major policy shift, the government has decided to convert all Preferential/Free Trade Agreements (PFA/FTA) into Comprehensive Economic Cooperation Agreements (CECA). This goes beyond the Indian government's bid in recent months to embrace bilateralism aggressively. The decision seems to be aimed at mollifying the World Trade Organization (WTO), which cautioned India against negotiating exclusively PFAs/FTAs. PTAs/FTAs usually involve structured reduction in tariffs between two countries. CECAs would cover preferential relaxation of FDI rules vis-à-vis the partner country, tax holidays on investment and income, easing of visa restrictions etc. Trade in services too would come under the purview of CECA.

Chapter 7: Investment Climate

Overview of Foreign Investment Climate

India's sizeable and rapidly growing domestic market, English-speaking population, and stable democratic government contribute to its being one of UNCTAD's 2010-12 top five destinations for foreign investment. Stock and commodity exchanges generally are well regulated by the relevant authorities. Despite these positive attributes, India continues to fare poorly in international business rankings. The International Finance Corporation ranked India 132 out of 183 world economies in its "Doing Business 2012 " report, and the World Bank ranks it the world's sixth slowest country in terms of the number of days it takes to resolve a commercial investment dispute. The heightened concerns of domestic investors about India's business climate are seen in declining capital formation and growing outbound foreign direct investment (FDI). The UN noted in its December 2011 report that India's 2010 FDI inflows declined approximately 30 percent to USD 25 billion from USD 36 billion in 2009.

The Goldman Sachs employee who coined the phrase "BRIC" recently commented that India was the most disappointing of the BRIC countries, due to its poor record on productivity, foreign direct investment, and economic reforms. Companies with operations in India often say that, in viewing the domestic investment climate, one has to focus at the state-level and on medium- to long- term returns on investment. Investors should be prepared to face varying conditions among India's 28 states and seven union territories. Many policies are implemented at the sub-national level and are subject to differences in local-level political governance, regulations, taxation, labor relations, infrastructure, and quality of education. Although India prides itself on its rule of law, its courts have cases backlogged for years. There is a strong Indian cultural and historical preference toward economic self-sufficiency and a corresponding tendency toward industrial and trade policies that protect domestic production and manufacturing, agriculture, and other sectors. Indian conglomerates and high technology companies are gaining sophistication and prominence on the world stage. Certain industrial sectors, such as information technology, telecommunications, and engineering are widely recognized for their innovation and competitiveness in the global market.

There are two channels for foreign investment: the "automatic route" and the "government route." Under the "automatic route," the foreign investor or Indian company is not required to seek approval from the relevant central government agency or department (e.g., coal and lignite mining, power, industrial parks, petroleum and gas, and non-banking finance). Instead, the investor is expected to notify the Reserve Bank of India (RBI) of its investment via Form "FC (RBI)" within 30 days of inward receipts and the issuance of shares. Investments subject to government approval are described as taking the "government route," and approval from vested ministries and agencies is required prior to the investment being transacted. The rules regulating government approval for investment in selected sectors vary from industry to industry and change frequently.

The approving entity also varies depending on the applicant and the product:

The Ministry of Commerce and Industry's (MOCI) Department of Industrial Policy and Promotion (DIPP) oversees single-brand product retailing investment proposals, as well as proposals made by Non- Resident Indians (NRIs), and Overseas Corporate Bodies (OCBs). An OCB is a company, partnership firm, or other corporate entity that is at least 60 percent owned, directly or indirectly, by NRIs, including overseas trusts.

The MOCI's Department of Commerce oversees proposals from export-oriented units (i.e., industrial companies that intend to export their entire production of goods and services from India abroad).

The Ministry of Finance's Foreign Investment Promotion Board (FIPB) oversees all other applications.

India has taken gradual steps toward FDI liberalization but the process has slowed in recent years. Industrial policy reforms have also stagnated. The GOI released its long-awaited National Manufacturing Policy in the fall of 2011. The policy framework is intended to be implemented by the states and line ministries and establishes National Investment and Manufacturing Zones (NIMZ) in an effort to better enable manufacturing and attract foreign investment. FDI policy is governed by the Foreign Exchange.

In India, an NRI can invest in the capital of a resident entity in certain sectors, but is subject to investment limits. According to

MOCI, a company with foreign investment that is majority-owned or controlled by resident Indians is authorized "downstream" investment without the transaction counting toward FDI caps on the part of the receiving entity or sector. In contrast, downstream investment by foreign- owned and foreign-controlled entities counts pro-rata towards FDI caps. (Note: For this purpose, NRIs are considered foreign.) This regulation results in the government counting foreign shareholding as domestic shareholding, so long as the investment is transacted via a shell company with only 49 percent foreign ownership.

Of note is that the GOI no longer differentiates between portfolio and direct investment in calculating foreign ownership. As a result, several large firms, particularly banks that have low FDI but high foreign portfolio holdings now find themselves in possible breach of foreign ownership limits. Under this definition, MOCI maintains that India's two largest banks, ICICI Bank and HDFC Bank, cannot be called Indian-owned banks. Foreign investors hold 77 percent equity in ICICI and 64 percent in HDFC. MOCI maintains that ICICI and HDFC Bank have violated the norms governing FDI in the country; however, banking analysts say the rules are confusing. Foreign investment is prohibited in many areas or subsectors such as: agriculture, real estate, multi-brand retailing, legal services, security services, atomic energy, railway transport, gambling, casinos, lotteries, cigars, cigarettes and tobacco substitutes, and trading in transferable development rights.

In November 2011, the Cabinet decided to lift the ban on multi-brand retail and raise the cap on single brand retail from 51 percent to 100 percent. Some of the political parties within the ruling United Progressive Alliance joined the opposition to oppose the decision, resulting in senior officials within the Congress party pledging not to move forward on the decision until greater political consensus is achieved. The Prime Minister, in late December, said the GOI will take up the multi-brand retail issue again after the Uttar Pradesh state elections end in March 2012.

In January 2012, DIPP announced it will now allow up to 100 percent FDI in single-brand retail, as long as companies source at least 30 percent of the total value of their products sold from Indian small- or micro-sized enterprise (SMEs). In July 2010, the DIPP issued a discussion paper regarding a proposal to raise the FDI cap in the defense sector from 26 percent to 74 percent. No change appears imminent. The GOI's privatization and disinvestment policy permits foreign investors to bid on the sale of state-owned enterprises. Foreign investors are given national treatment at the time of initial investment. Obligations and local content requirements are imposed on foreign investors in certain industries.

Existing foreign and domestic companies can also use the automatic route for additional FDI, provided the sector falls under the automatic route. These companies need to notify the relevant authorities of their expansion plans and must use funds from abroad rather than funds leveraged from the domestic market. The Indian company's Board of Directors must approve such investments.

Sector-Specific Guidelines for FDI in key industries (alphabetical order):

Advertising and Film: One hundred percent FDI via the automatic route is allowed in the advertising and film industries, which includes film production, exhibition, distribution, and related services and products.

Agriculture: No FDI is permitted in farming, except tea plantations. Foreigners are not authorized to own farmland. FDI in agriculture-related activities such as the seed industry, floriculture, horticulture, animal husbandry, aquaculture, fish farming, and cultivation of vegetables and mushrooms is permitted without limits under the automatic route. For tea plantations, 100 percent FDI is allowed via the government route. However, there is a compulsory divestment of 26 percent equity in favor of the Indian partner or potential Indian investors within five years from the date the FDI enters the country. In other plantation sectors, no FDI is allowed.

Airline Carriers: With domestic airlines experiencing financial difficulties, the Indian government announced in January 2012 that it will open the sector to allow foreign air carriers to invest up to 49 percent in Indian air carriers. The policy has yet to be formally enacted. FDI by foreign carriers currently stands at zero.

Airport Infrastructure: One hundred percent FDI is allowed in greenfield projects through the automatic route. FDI up to 74 percent is allowed in existing projects through the automatic route; FDI greater than 74 percent requires FIPB approval. Foreign companies can own up to 74 percent of the ground-handling businesses at airports, with 49 percent via the automatic route; FDI from 49 percent to 74 percent is permitted via the government route. NRIs are allowed 100 percent FDI in ground-handling services. One hundred percent FDI is allowed through the automatic route for maintenance and repair operations, flight training institutes, and technical training institutes.

Airport Transport Services: FDI is limited to 49 percent under the automatic route for air transport services, including domestic scheduled passenger airlines. For non-scheduled, chartered, and/or cargo airlines, the FDI limit is 74 percent. For helicopter and seaplane services, 100 percent FDI is allowed on automatic approval – meaning FIPB is not involved – but requires formal approval by the Directorate General of Civil Aviation. NRIs may own 100 percent of a domestic airline. Although frequently debated, India has yet to open its state-run international airlines to outside investment. The U.S.-India "Open Skies" agreement, signed in April 2005, allows unrestricted access by U.S. carriers to the Indian market and vice-versa.

Alcoholic Distillation and Brewing: One hundred percent FDI is allowed through the automatic route but still requires a license via DIPP under the provisions of the Industries (Development and Regulation) Act, 1951.

Asset Reconstruction Companies: FDI is limited to 49 percent via the government route. No portfolio investment is allowed. Where any individual investment exceeds 10 percent of the equity, the approval is subject to the Securitization and

Reconstruction of Financial Assets and Enforcement of Security Interest (SARFAESI) Act, 2002.

Automobiles: No FDI caps, local content requirements, or export obligations apply. FDI in automobile manufacturing is allowed under the automatic approval route.

Banking: Aggregate foreign investment from all sources in all private banks is capped at 74 percent. For state-owned banks, the foreign ownership limit is 20 percent. According to the 2011 road map for foreign bank entry, there are three distinct ways to enter the Indian banking sector. The first is by establishing a branch in India. The second is to establish a wholly-owned subsidiary, though it is important to note that foreign banks are permitted to have either branches or subsidiaries but not both. The third is to establish a subsidiary with total foreign investment of up to 74 percent. Foreign investors are also allowed to acquire an ailing bank, except the RBI has never authorized this type of transaction. Institutional investors (FII) can invest in a bank up to 10 percent of the total paid-up capital and 5 percent in cases where the FII is a foreign bank/bank group. Voting rights in private banks and state-owned banks are currently capped at 10 percent and 1 percent, respectively, and do not represent ownership. The Banking Regulation (Amendment) Bill, which would align voting rights in private banks with shareholding, remains in a Parliamentary committee and has yet to be introduced.

Broadcasting: Foreign investment – FDI, NRI, persons of Indian origin, and portfolio investment – is limited to 20 percent in frequency modulation terrestrial broadcasting, via the government approval route, and is subject to guidelines issued by the Ministry of Information and Broadcasting. For direct-to-home broadcasting, foreign investment from all sources is limited to 49 percent, with an additional caveat limiting the maximum FDI component to 20 percent with the remainder provided by NRI and/or portfolio investment. In satellite broadcasting, foreign investment – FDI, NRI, persons of Indian origin and portfolio investment – is limited to 49 percent via the government approval route. TV channels, irrespective of ownership or management control, have to up-link from India and comply with the broadcast code issued by the Ministry of Information and Broadcasting. FDI is limited to 26 percent, including portfolio investment, in news and current affairs channels up-linking from India. One hundred percent FDI is permitted in entertainment and general interest channels. FDI up to 49 percent is permitted via the government approval route for establishing up-linking hub/teleports.

Business Services: One hundred percent FDI is allowed under the automatic route in data processing, software development, and computer consultancy services. One hundred percent FDI is allowed for call centers and business processing outsourcing (BPO) organizations, subject to certain conditions. Cable Network: FDI and portfolio investment is limited to 49 percent, including both FDI and portfolio investment. Prior approval is required, subject to Cable Television Networks Rules, 1994.

Coal/Lignite: FDI up to 100 percent is allowed, via the automatic route, in private Indian companies that have captive coal or lignite mines for either direct power generation or for captive consumption in their iron/steel/cement production plants. Similarly, 100 percent foreign investment in the equity of either an Indian company or the Indian subsidiary of a foreign company is allowed for setting up coal processing plants, subject to the conditions that the equity recipient shall not engage in coal mining or sell washed (processed) coal from such plants in the open market.

Coffee and Rubber Processing and Warehousing: One hundred percent FDI is permitted under the automatic route with no conditions.

Commodity Exchanges: Foreign ownership up to 49 percent, with portfolio investment limited to 23 percent and FDI limited to 26 percent, is allowed via the government route. FII purchases shall be restricted to secondary markets only and no single foreign investor/entity can hold more than five percent of the total paid-up capital.

Construction Development Projects: FDI is permitted up to 100 percent in the construction and maintenance of roads, highways, vehicular bridges, tunnels, ports and harbors, townships, housing, commercial buildings, resorts, educational institutions, and infrastructure. Automatic approval is subject to certain minimum capitalization and minimum area-of-development requirements. Since 2010, the minimum capitalization requirement has been USD 10 million for wholly owned subsidiaries and USD 5 million for joint ventures with Indian partners. In the case of serviced housing plots, a minimum of 10 hectares (25 acres) must be developed, while in the case of construction-development projects, the minimum built-up area must be 50,000 square meters (approx. 538,000 square feet). At least 50 percent of the project must be developed within five years from the date of obtaining all statutory clearances.

Credit Information Companies: Foreign investment is permitted up to 49 percent and is subject to FIPB and RBI approval. Portfolio investment is limited to 24 percent and no single investor/entity can hold more than 10 percent of the total paid-up capital. Furthermore, any acquisition in excess of one percent requires mandatory reporting to RBI.

Courier Services (Other Than Distribution of Letters): One hundred per cent FDI is permitted; however, FIPB approval is required.

Defense and Strategic Industries: FDI is limited to 26 percent and is subject to a DIPP license in consultation with the Defense Ministry. Production of arms and ammunition is subject to additional FDI guidelines. There are no automatic approvals. Purchase and price preferences may be given to Public Sector Enterprises as per Department of Public Enterprise guidelines. The licensee must establish adequate safety and security procedures once the authorization is granted and production begins.

Drugs/Pharmaceuticals: In October 2011, FDI rules were changed for the pharmaceutical sector. For greenfield investments, 100 percent FDI will continue to be allowed.

However, in case of brown-field investments, FDI will be allowed through the FIPB through April 2012. It is expected that, by April 2012, regulations for mergers and acquisitions will be put in place by the Competition Commission of India (CCI) that will ensure a balance between public health concerns and FDI. Thereafter, FDI oversight for brown-field investments will be done by the CCI in accordance with India's competition (i.e., antitrust) laws.

E-commerce: FDI up to 100 percent is allowed in business-to-business e-commerce under the government approval route. No FDI is allowed in retail e-commerce.

Education Services: FDI is permitted up to 100 percent in education services via the automatic route, but only in collaboration with an Indian partner. A bill pending in Parliament would, if passed, allow foreign universities to establish campuses independently without working with an Indian partner institution, but with conditions attached.

Food Processing: FDI is allowed up to 100 percent with automatic approval for: fruit and vegetable processing, dairy products, meat and poultry products, fishing and fish processing, grains, confections, consumer and convenience foods, soft bottling, food parks, cold chain, and warehousing. The exception is for alcoholic beverages and beer, where a license is required, and items reserved for the small-scale sector. FDI up to 100 percent is allowed via the automatic route for cold storage facilities.

Hazardous chemicals: FDI is allowed up to 100 percent via the automatic route. However, a DIPP license is required under the provisions of the Industries (Development and Regulation) Act, 1951.

Health Services: FDI is allowed up to 100 percent under the automatic route.

Hotels, Tourism, and Restaurants: FDI up to 100 percent is allowed with automatic approval.

Housing/Real Estate: No FDI is permitted in the retail housing sector by foreigners. However, NRIs who can obtain "Overseas Citizenship of India" status are allowed to own property and invest in India as if they were citizens. NRIs may invest up to 100 percent FDI with prior government approval in the real estate sector and in integrated townships including housing, commercial premises, resorts, and hotels, as well as in projects such as the manufacture of building materials.

Industrial explosives: FDI at 100 percent via the automatic route is allowed, subject to licensing by the appropriate authorities.

Industrial Parks: FDI up to 100 percent under the automatic route is allowed, provided that the industrial park includes at least ten units with no single unit occupying more than 50 percent of the area, and at least 66 percent of the area is made available for industrial activity.

Information Technology: FDI of 100 percent is allowed with automatic approval in software and electronics, except in the aerospace and defense sectors.

Insurance: FDI is limited to 26 percent in insurance and insurance brokering. While FDI approval is automatic, the Insurance Regulatory and Development Authority (IRDA) must first grant a license. The debate over raising the cap on FDI in insurance continues, after more than four years of consideration in Parliament. It remains unclear as to whether the investment cap will increase in this sector.

Infrastructure Companies in the Securities Market (i.e., stock exchanges, depositories, and clearing corporations): Foreign investment is capped at 49 percent via the government route. FDI is limited to 26 percent and FIIs are limited to 23 percent. Regarding stock exchanges specifically, total foreign investment, including portfolio investment, is allowed via the government route (via FIPB) up to 49 percent.

Legal services: No FDI is allowed, and recent court cases have sought to limit the ability of foreign attorneys to provide legal services here. Most foreign attorneys practice in India as legal consultants. In March 2010, a writ of petition was filed by a Chennai-based attorney on behalf of the Association of Indian Lawyers against 31 foreign law firms, the Bar Council of India, and the Ministry of External Affairs in the Madras High Court, seeking to prevent foreign law firms from practicing in India. A similar case was decided against foreign firms in December 2009, in the Bombay High Court. The Madras High Court has repeatedly delayed a decision in order to give the court more time to consult with foreign firms. The implications of these cases are unclear and the status of foreign law firms remains uncertain. The petitioner in the Madras case and other opponents to market liberalization insist U.S. attorneys should be barred from practicing law in India until there is reciprocity in the U.S. market.

Lottery, Gambling, and Betting: No FDI of any form is allowed.

Manufacturing: The new National Manufacturing Policy encourages greater local content requirements for Governmentprocurementincertainsectors. Government approval is required for any foreign investment greater than 24 percent equity when the manufacturer is not a small- or micro-sized enterprise (SME) and the entity will manufacture items reserved for the SME sector [Note: An SME is defined as a company having total investment in plant and machinery worth under USD 1 million.]. Manufacturers in this category are subject to additional licensing and minimum export requirements. Since 1997, the government has been steadily decreasing the number of industry sectors reserved under the small scale industry (SSI) policy, from a peak of 800 industries in the late 1990s, to just 21 specific goods/services today.

Mining: FDI up to 100 percent is allowed, with automatic approval for diamonds and precious stones, gold/silver, and other mineral mining and exploration. FDI up to 100 percent is also allowed for mining and mineral separation of titanium minerals and ores, but such activity requires prior government approval.

Non-Banking Financial Companies (NBFC): FDI is allowed up to 100 percent via the automatic route. In India, NBFCs include: merchant banking, underwriting, portfolio management, financial consulting, stockbrokerage, asset management, venture capital, credit rating agencies, housing finance, leasing and finance, credit card businesses, foreign exchange brokerages, money changers, factoring and custodial services, investment advisory services, and micro and rural credit. All investments are subject to the following minimum capitalization norms: USD 500,000 upfront for investments with up to 51 percent foreign ownership; USD 5 million upfront for investments with 51 percent to 74.9 percent ownership; USD 50 million total, with USD 7.5 million required up-front and the remaining balance within 24 months, for investments with more than 75 percent ownership. One hundred percent foreign-owned NBFCs, with a minimum capitalization of USD 50 million, are not restricted as to the number of subsidiaries established for specific NBFC activities and are not required to bring in additional capital. Joint-venture operating NBFCs with up to 75 percent foreign investment are allowed to set up subsidiaries for other NBFC activities and are also subject to the minimum capitalization norms.

Pensions: No FDI is allowed in the pension sector. The Pension Fund Development and Regulatory Authority Bill 2011, which cleared a Parliamentary standing committee in August 2011, would establish a regulator for pensions and empower it with the authority to set FDI caps, among other powers. The timing for passage remains unclear.

Petroleum: FDI limits, along with tax incentives, production sharing, and other terms and conditions apply, although investment is authorized via the automatic route with some sub-sector specific variance, such as:

- Discovered small fields: 100 percent - Refining with domestic private company: 100 percent - Refining by public sector company*: 49 percent

- Petroleum product/pipeline: 100 percent

- Petrol/diesel retail outlets: 100 percent

- LNG Pipeline: 100 percent

- Exploration: 100 percent

- Investment Financing: 100 percent

- Market study and formulation: 100 percent

(* Requires FIPB approval and disinvestment is prohibited.)

Pollution Control: FDI up to 100 percent is allowed with automatic approval for equipment manufacture and for consulting and management services.

Ports and harbors: FDI up to 100 percent with automatic approval is allowed in construction and manufacturing of ports and harbors. FDI up to 100 percent is allowed in the port sector to supplement domestic capital, technology, and skills, in order to accelerate economic growth. The Union Minister of Shipping clarified that security clearances from the Ministry of Defense are required for all bidders on port projects, and only the bids of cleared bidders will be considered.

Power: FDI up to 100 percent is permitted with automatic approval in projects related to electricity generation, transmission, distribution, power trading, and renewable energy. The exception is nuclear reactor power plants, where private sector ownership, both domestic and foreign, is currently prohibited.

Print Media: Foreign investment in newspapers and news periodicals is restricted to 26 percent under the government approval route. FDI is permitted up to 100 percent in printing science and technology magazines/journals, subject to prior government approval and guidelines issued by the Ministry of Information and Broadcasting.

Professional services: FDI is limited to 51 percent in most consulting and professional services, with automatic approval. Legal services, however, are not open to foreign investment.

Research and Development Services: One hundred percent FDI is allowed under the automatic route.

Railways: FDI is not allowed in train operations, although 100 percent FDI is permitted in auxiliary areas such as rail track construction, ownership of rolling stock, provisioning of container services, and container depots.

Retailing: In January 2012, DIPP announced that it will now allow up to 100 percent FDI in single-brand retail, as long as companies source at least 30 percent of the total value of their products sold from Indian SMEs.

FDI in multi-brand retail continues to be prohibited. Several large multinational retailers have successfully partnered with Indian companies to form joint-venture wholesale enterprises to avoid violating FDI prohibitions. The GOI plans to reconsider allowing FDI up to 51 percent in multi-brand retail after state elections in spring 2012, and once it has gathered greater state-government and political party support for such a move.

Roads, Highways, and Mass Rapid Transport Systems: FDI up to 100 percent is allowed with automatic approval for construction and maintenance.

Satellites: FDI is limited to 74 percent for the establishment and operation of satellites, with prior government approval.

Security Agencies: Foreign shareholding is restricted to a maximum of 49 percent under the government approval route.

Shipping: FDI is limited to 74 percent with automatic approval for water transport services.

Special Economic Zones (SEZ): FDI up to 100 percent is allowed automatically when establishing a SEZ and an individual unit within a SEZ. Establishing the unit is subject to the Special Economic Zones Act, 2005, and MOCI regulations.

Storage and Warehouse Services: FDI up to 100 percent is allowed under the automatic route, including warehousing of agricultural products with cold storage.

Telecommunications: This sector is considered sensitive by the GOI and therefore foreign investment is carefully scrutinized and controlled. FDI in the telecom services sector can be made directly or indirectly in the operating company or through a holding company, subject to licensing and security requirements. DIPP sets the security conditions that prospective investors must follow to participate in the telecom sector. When approving investment proposals, FIPB will note whether the investment is coming from countries of concern or unfriendly countries. FDI in telecom services such as basic, cellular, access services, national/international long distance, VSat public mobile radio trunked services, global mobile, unified personal communication services, ISP gateways, radio-paging, and end-to-end services is limited to 74 percent, and FDI proposals above 49 percent must go via the government route. FDI up to 100 percent is allowed in equipment manufacturing via the automatic route. FDI in internet service providers (ISP) with and without international gateways, including those for satellite and marine cables, is limited to 74 percent, of which 49 percent is allowed via the automatic route. Infrastructure providers providing fiber-optic, right-of- way, duct space, voice mail, and email are allowed up to 100 percent. In both cases, 26 percent divestment is required within the first five years of the investment.

Trading/Wholesale: FDI of 100 percent is allowed through the automatic route for activities such as exporting, bulk imports with export warehouse sales, and cash-and-carry wholesale trading. A wholesaler/cash-and-carry trader cannot open a retail shop to sell directly to consumers. In the case of test marketing, or if the items are sourced from the small-scale sector, FIPB approval is required. Single-brand retailing is allowed subject to FIPB approval and the FDI limit is now 100 percent, as long as companies source at least 30 percent of the total value of their products sold from Indian SMEs.

Conversion and Transfer Policies

The Indian rupee is fully convertible for current account transactions, which are regulated under the Foreign Exchange Management Rules, 2000. Prior RBI approval is required for acquiring foreign currency above certain limits for specific purposes (e.g., foreign travel, consulting services, and foreign studies). Capital account transactions are open for foreign investors and subject to various clearances. In recent years, with growing foreign exchange reserves, the Indian government has taken additional steps to relax foreign exchange and capital account controls for Indian companies and individuals. For example, since 2007, individuals are permitted to transfer up to USD 200,000 per year abroad for any purpose without approval.

The GOI now allows all NRI proposals for conversion of non-repatriable equity into repatriable equity under the automatic approval route. On December 19, 2011, the exchange rate was Rupees 52.93 to USD 1, compared to Rupees 45.3 and 46.7 at the end of 2010 and 2009, respectively. The crisis in Europe and a worsening domestic outlook are the principal drivers of the rupee's decline. Some analysts view the rupee's two-month decline against the dollar as being cyclical and predict that next year the currency will appreciate if inflation slows and growth recovers.

NRI investment in real estate may be subject to a "lock-in" period. There are no restrictions on remittances for debt service or payments for imported inputs. Profits and dividend remittances, as current account transactions, are permitted without RBI approval but income tax payment clearance is required. There are generally no transfer delays beyond 60 days. RBI approval is needed to remit funds from asset liquidation. Foreign partners may sell their shares to resident Indian investors without RBI approval, provided the shares were held on a repatriation basis.

Global Depository Receipts and American Depository Receipts proceeds from abroad may be retained without restrictions except for an end-use ban on investment in real estate and stock markets. FIPB approval is required for converting non-repatriable shares to repatriable ones. Up to USD 1 million per year may be remitted for transfer of assets into India. Foreign institutional investors (FII) may transfer funds from rupee to foreign currency accounts and vice- versa at the market exchange rate. They may also repatriate capital, capital gains, dividends, interest income, and any compensation from the sale of rights offerings, net of all taxes, without RBI approval. The RBI authorizes automatic approval to Indian industries for foreign collaboration agreements, royalty, and lump sum fees for transfer of technology and payments for the use of trademark and brand names with no limits. Royalties and lump sum payments are taxed at ten percent. Foreign banks may remit profits and surpluses to their headquarters, subject to the banks' compliance with the Banking Regulation Act, 1949. Banks are permitted to offer foreign currency-rupee swaps without limits to enable customers to hedge their foreign currency liabilities. They may also offer forward cover to non- resident entities on FDI deployed after 1993.

Expropriation and Compensation

Dispute Settlement

Foreign investors frequently complain about a lack of "sanctity of contracts." According to the World Bank, India continues to be the sixth slowest country in the world in the number of days it takes to resolve a dispute. Indian courts are understaffed and lack the technology to address the backlog of unsettled cases. According to the World Bank's "Doing Business 2011" report, it takes about seven years to liquidate a business in India. In an attempt to align its adjudication of commercial contract disputes with the rest of the world, India enacted the Arbitration and Conciliation Act, 1996, based on the UNCITRAL (United Nations Commission on International Trade Law) model. Foreign awards are enforceable under multilateral conventions like the Geneva Convention.

The Indian government established the International Center for Alternative Dispute Resolution (ICADR) as an autonomous organization under the Ministry of Law and Justice to promote the settlement of domestic and international disputes through alternate dispute resolution. The World Bank funded ICADR to conduct training for mediators in commercial disputes settlement. India is a member of the New York Convention of 1958 on the Recognition and Enforcement of Foreign Arbitral Awards. India has yet to become a member of the International Center for the Settlement of Investment Disputes. The Permanent Court of Arbitration (PCA, The Hague) and the Indian Law Ministry agreed, in 2007, to establish a regional PCA office in New Delhi to provide an arbitration forum to match the facilities offered at The Hague at a far lower cost. Since then, no further progress has been made in establishing such an office.

In late November 2011, while speaking to The Indian Express on the sidelines of a special lecture he delivered at the Indian Society of International Law, Brooks W. Daly – Deputy Secretary- General and Principal Legal Counsel of the Permanent Court of Arbitration hearing the Kishanganga water dispute between India and Pakistan – said the court was seeking "more representation around the world" and also did not rule out a permanent representative in India. In November 2009, the Department of Revenue's Central Board of Direct Taxes established eight dispute resolution panels (DRPs) across the country to settle the transfer-pricing tax disputes of domestic and foreign companies in a faster and more cost-effective manner.

Performance Requirements and Incentives

The government is currently considering local content requirements to promote the development of a domestic manufacturing base, although the final policies and regulations have yet to be notified.

Plant Location: Companies are free to select the location of their industrial projects. An earlier restriction prohibiting location of factories near urban settlements was lifted in July 2008; however, projects still require clearance from the state's pollution board environment ministry.

Employment: There is no requirement to employ Indian nationals. Restrictions on employing foreign technicians and managers were eliminated, though companies complain that hiring and compensating expatriates is time consuming and expensive. The RBI permits remittances at a per-diem rate up to USD 1,000, with an annual ceiling of USD 200,000, for services provided by foreign workers payable to a foreign firm. Employment of foreigners in excess of 12 months requires approval from the Ministry of Home Affairs (MHA). The Department of Telecommunications under the Ministry of Communications and Information Technology regulates the employment of foreign nationals in the telecom sector due to national security concerns.

Majority Directors, but not necessarily stakeholders, serving on the boards of telecom companies, including the Chairman, Managing Director, Chief Executive Officer, and Chief Financial Officer, must be Indian citizens. The Chief-Officer in charge of technical network operations and the Chief Security Officer should be resident Indian citizens. The positions of Chairman, Chief Executive Officer, and Chief Financial Officer, if held by foreign nationals, require annual security clearance vetting by MHA. In August 2009, the government tightened employment visa and business rules for foreigners.

Foreign nationals executing projects/contracts in India now require "employment" visas. The government only issues "business" visas to individuals entering India to explore business opportunities, set up a business, or sell industrial products. Furthermore, in the wake of disclosures about the abuse of tourist visas by Pakistani-American terror suspect David Headley, MHA decided that foreign nationals having a multi-entry Indian tourist visa must wait a minimum of two months between visits to India. Additional visits within the two month period may be allowed if the visa holder can provide an itinerary for a regional trip. The two-month gap restriction does not apply to Persons of Indian Origin or Overseas Citizen of India card-holders, or to foreigners holding business, employment, student, and other categories of visa. There continues to be widespread confusion and inconsistent application of these rules. In view of these concerns, the government eased tourist norms for foreign nationals from Finland, Japan, Luxembourg, New Zealand, Singapore, Cambodia, Laos, and Vietnam through the MHArun visa-on-demand scheme.

Taxes: The GOI provides a 10-year tax holiday for knowledge-based start-ups. Most state governments also offer fiscal concessions to almost all industries. Large fiscal deficits at the state and central government level, along with attempts to reform both the direct and indirect tax regimes throughout India, have increased uncertainty about investors' tax liability. In a few high-profile lawsuits now pending appeal, Indian tax collectors have made significant tax assessments on mergers and acquisitions by large multinationals in cases where the acquisition was made outside of India. Press reports have noted increasing investor concern about the lack of transparency and predictability in India's taxation of mergers and acquisitions.

The central government is leaning towards rationalizing the tax structure and simplifying the tax code. The UPA government started a country-wide campaign in favor of lowering tax rates, reducing the number of exceptions, and creating greater transparency in tax administration, but has met significant opposition. The Central and state governments continue to consider implementing a national Goods and Services Tax (GST) to rationalize the current, indirect tax system. The idea behind GST is to standardize taxes levied at all points in the supply chain concurrently by both the central and state governments. A GST would replace national and state Value-Added Taxes (VATs), central excise taxes, and a number of other state-level taxes. The central and state governments, during the Budget session of Parliament in March 2011, agreed to an initial list that did not include contentious items such as fuel and liquor in order to allow the Cabinet to clear a Constitutional amendment requirement to implement GST.

As of the Parliament's December 2011 Winter Session, the Constitutional Amendment was awaiting passage. MOCI develops incentives for exporters to boost their exports. In August 2009, MOCI released its foreign trade policy for fiscal years 2009-14, which highlighted various incentives for exporters with a particular emphasis on employment-generating sectors such as textiles, processed foods, leather, gems and jewelry, tea, and handloom-made items. Under this policy, the GOI added 26 new markets, including 16 Latin American countries and 10 in Asia-Oceania. The duty credit extended to exporters under this scheme is three percent of the free-on-board (FOB) export value. Furthermore, exporters can import machinery and capital goods at concessional duty rates, which currently stand at zero. Exporters are allowed to use the duty cash reimbursement scheme, which neutralized duties paid on inputs by exporters through June 30, 2011. India's tax exemption for profits from export earnings has been completely phased out.

Right to Private Ownership and Establishment

Foreign and domestic private entities are allowed to establish and own businesses in trading companies, subsidiaries, joint ventures, branch offices, project offices, and liaison offices, subject to certain sector- specific restrictions. The GOI does not permit investment in real estate by foreign investors, except for company property used to do business and for the development of most types of new commercial and residential properties. FIIs can now invest in Initial Public Offerings (IPOs) of companies engaged in real estate. They can also participate in pre-IPO placements undertaken by such real estate companies without regard to FDI stipulations.

To establish a business, various government approvals and clearances are required including incorporation of the company and registration under the State Sales Tax Act and Central and State Excise Acts. Businesses that intend to own land and build facilities are also required to: register the land; seek land use permission when the industry is located outside an industrially zoned area; obtain environmental site approval; seek authorization for electricity and financing; and obtain appropriate approvals for construction plans from the respective state and municipal authorities. Promoters also need to obtain industry-specific environmental approvals in compliance with the Water and Air Pollution Control Acts. Petrochemical complexes, petroleum refineries, cement thermal power plants, bulk drug makers, and manufacturers of fertilizers, dyes, and paper, among others, must obtain clearance from the Ministry of Environment and Forests. The GOI passed the Securitization Act in 2002, to introduce bankruptcy laws. The requirement to obtain government permission before shutting down some businesses, however, makes it difficult to dispose of company assets. Parliament is currently considering the third iteration of a modernization of India's bankruptcy and corporate governance bills, The Companies Bill, 2011.

Protection of Property Rights

India has generally adequate copyright laws, but enforcement is weak and piracy of copyrighted materials is widespread. India is a party to the Berne Convention, Geneva Phonograms Convention, and the Universal Copyright Convention, and is a member of both UNESCO and the World Intellectual Property Organization (WIPO), though the country has not yet signed and incorporated into domestic law the WIPO Internet treaties. The government has set up one exclusive bench for hearing intellectual property (IP) cases in the Karnataka High Court. India has yet to fully modernize legislation addressing copyright and intellectual property protections. The Ministry of Human Resource Development considered and amended the draft bill based on the 2010 Parliamentary Standing Committee's recommendations and sought to re-introduce it during the 2011 November- December Winter Session of Parliament.

Unfortunately, the edited bill has met with opposition based on allegations of "conflict of interest" against the Minister of Human Resource Development himself and the bill has not made much progress. The Copyright Amendment Bill, 2011, contains provisions to deal with technology issues by extending protection of copyrighted material in India over digital networks related to literary, dramatic, musical and artistic works, films, and sound recordings. The bill also seeks to provide clauses for stringent punishment for copyright violations. In October 2010, the government, along with the Federation of Indian Chambers of Commerce and Industry (FICC), set up an Anti-Piracy Coordination Cell web portal, which will function as a centralized agency to curb piracy, thus fulfilling India's "zero tolerance" commitment.

In August 2010, Parliament passed the Trade Marks (Amendment) Bill, 2009, which brings India into greater compliance with international standards for filing and granting trademarks. The law makes it easier for Indian and foreign nationals to secure simultaneous protection of trademarks in other countries. Through a single application, a person or enterprise can register a trademark in any of the 84 member countries of the Madrid Protocol. Before this law, applicants had to approach different countries in different languages, each with a separate fee. This system of trademark application filing under the Madrid Protocol is expected to be implemented by the Indian Intellectual Property Office in 2012. Pharmaceutical and agro-chemical products can be patented in India. Software embedded in hardware may also be patented. However, the interpretation and application of the law lacks clarity, especially with regard to several important areas such as compulsory license triggers, pre-grant opposition provisions, and defining the scope of patentable inventions (e.g., whether patents are limited to new chemical entities rather than incremental innovation).

India also provides protection for plant varieties through the Plant Varieties and Farmers' Rights Act, 2001. Indian law does not protect against the unfair commercial use of test data or other data submitted to the government during the application for market approval of pharmaceutical or agro-chemical products. The Pesticides Management Bill, 2008, which would allow data protection of agricultural chemical provisions, was introduced in Parliament in October 2008, and thereafter referred to the Standing Committee on Agriculture, which subsequently submitted recommendations to Parliament. As of December 2011, these recommendations had been examined by the Ministry of Agriculture and the amended draft is expected to be re-introduced soon in the Parliament. Indian law provides no statutory protection of trade secrets. The Designs Act, 2000, meets India's obligations under the TRIPS (Trade-Related Aspects of Intellectual Property Rights) Agreement for industrial designs. The Design Rules, 2008, which detail classification of design, conform to the international system and are intended to take care of the proliferation of design-related activities in various fields. India's Semiconductor Integrated Circuits Layout Designs Act, 2000, is based on standards developed by WIPO. However, this law remains inactive due to the lack of implementing regulations.

Right to Private Ownership and Establishment

Foreign and domestic private entities are allowed to establish and own businesses in trading companies, subsidiaries, joint ventures, branch offices, project offices, and liaison offices, subject to certain sector- specific restrictions. The GOI does not permit investment in real estate by foreign investors, except for company property used to do business and for the development of most types of new commercial and residential properties. FIIs can now invest in Initial Public Offerings (IPOs) of companies engaged in real estate. They can also participate in pre-IPO placements undertaken by such real estate companies without regard to FDI stipulations.

To establish a business, various government approvals and clearances are required including incorporation of the company and registration under the State Sales Tax Act and Central and State Excise Acts. Businesses that intend to own land and build facilities are also required to: register the land; seek land use permission when the industry is located outside an industrially zoned area; obtain environmental site approval; seek authorization for electricity and financing; and obtain appropriate approvals for construction plans from the respective state and municipal authorities. Promoters also need to obtain industry-specific environmental approvals in compliance with the Water and Air Pollution Control Acts. Petrochemical complexes, petroleum refineries, cement thermal power plants, bulk drug makers, and manufacturers of fertilizers, dyes, and paper, among others, must obtain clearance from the Ministry of Environment and Forests.

The GOI passed the Securitization Act in 2002, to introduce bankruptcy laws. The requirement to obtain government permission before shutting down some businesses, however, makes it difficult to dispose of company assets. Parliament is currently considering the third iteration of a modernization of India's bankruptcy and corporate governance bills, The Companies Bill, 2011.

Transparency of Regulatory System

Despite progress, the Indian economy is still constrained by excessive rules and a powerful bureaucracy with broad discretionary powers. India has a decentralized federal system of government in which states possess extensive regulatory powers. Regulatory decisions governing important issues such as zoning, land-use, and the environment vary between states. Opposition from labor unions and political constituencies slows the pace of reform in exit policy, bankruptcy, and labor rights. The Central government has been successful in establishing independent and effective regulators in telecommunications, securities, insurance, and pensions.

The Competition Commission of India (CCI), India's antitrust body, has started using its enforcement powers and is now taking cases against cartelization and abuse of dominance, as well as conducting capacity-building programs. In June 2011, the government enacted rules governing mergers and acquisitions. The Securities and Exchange Bureau of India (SEBI) enforces corporate governance and is well regarded by foreign institutional investors. The Satyam Computer Services' (SCS) fraud case, in which the SCS chairman admitted that 94 percent of the company's USD 1 billion in cash was fictitious, led to several proposals for reform measures including: rotation of audit partners, additional disclosure requirements, and granting additional powers to a company's audit committee. Most of these proposed reforms are a part of the amendments to The Companies Bill, 2011, which was introduced in Parliament in December 2011.

Efficient Capital Markets and Portfolio Investment

Indian capital markets are growing. The combined market capitalizations of the Bombay Stock Exchange (BSE) and the National Stock Exchange (NSE) exceeded USD 2.2 trillion in mid-December 2011. As of November 2011, the Indian benchmark index Sensex had lost more than 21 percent while, at the same time, the rupee depreciated 17 percent. The combined effect of the market slide and rupee's depreciation led to a dip in India's market capitalization. Together, the NSE and BSE account for 100 percent of total stock market turnover. The NSE and BSE are the world's fourth and fifth largest stock exchanges in terms of transaction volume. They are smaller in comparison to foreign exchanges in terms of market capitalization.

Spot prices for index stocks are usually market-driven and settlement mechanisms are in line with international standards. India's debt and currency markets lag behind its equity markets. Although private placements of corporate debt have been increasing, daily trading volume remains low. Foreign portfolio investment and activities in India's capital markets are regulated by a complex and onerous foreign institutional investor (FII) regime, analogous to China's Qualified Foreign Institutional

Investor regime. The FII regime sets caps on investment and the scope of business. It reflects India' relatively closed capital account, the lack of market access for foreign firms, and the strict regulation of the financial sector. FIIs investing in India's capital markets must register with SEBI, India's Securities and Exchange Commission (SEC) equivalent. They are divided into two categories: regular FIIs, which invest in both equity and debt; and 100 percent debt-fund FIIs.

The list of eligible FIIs includes pension funds, mutual funds, banks, foreign central banks, sovereign wealth funds, endowment and university funds, foundations, charitable trusts and societies, insurance companies, re-insurance companies, foreign government agencies, international or multilateral organizations, broad-based funds, asset management companies, investment managers and hedge funds. FIIs must be registered and regulated by a recognized authority in their home country, meaning many US-based hedge funds cannot register as FIIs. FII registration can be made either as an investor or investor on behalf of its "accounts." "Sub-account" means any person residing outside India on whose behalf investments are made within India by an FII. As of March 2011, there are a total of 1,722 FIIs registered in India and 5,686 subaccounts. FIIs now hold 15 percent of the Indian stock market. FII outflow through December 14, 2011, totaled USD 331 million compared to an inflow of USD 29.36 billion in 2010. After the global financial crisis, FIIs withdrew USD 12.18 billion when they sold their shares of Indian companies.

While FIIs are allowed to invest in all securities traded on India's primary and secondary markets, in unlisted domestic debt securities, and in commercial paper issued by Indian companies, the GOI imposes some restrictions based on investment type. In November 2011, the GOI raised the investment limit for FIIs in government securities and corporate bonds by USD five billion each to USD 15 billion and USD 20 billion respectively. In corporate bonds, the limit of USD 20 billion is separate from the USD 25 billion allowed for long-term infrastructure bonds. In the equities market, FII and sub-accounts can own up to 10 percent and 5 percent, respectively, of the paid-up equity capital of any Indian company.

Aggregate investment in any Indian company by all FIIs and sub- accounts is also capped at 24 percent, unless specifically authorized by that company's board of directors. "Naked short selling" is not permitted. FIIs are not permitted to participate in the new currency futures markets. Foreign firms and persons are prohibited from trading in commodities. SEBI allows foreign brokers to work on behalf of registered FIIs. FIIs can also bypass brokers and deal directly with companies in open offers. FII bank deposits are fully convertible and their capital, capital gains, dividends, interest income, and any compensation from the sale of rights offerings, net of all taxes, may be repatriated without prior approval. NRIs are subject to separate investment limitations. They can repatriate dividends, rents, and interest earned in India and their specially designated bank deposits are fully convertible.

In August 2011, the government allowed qualified foreign investors (QFIs) to invest in the equity and debt schemes of mutual funds. In January 2012, the government announced it would allow QFIs to invest directly in equities. QFIs are defined as individuals, groups or associations that reside in a foreign country that is compliant with the Financial Action Task Force (FATF) and that is a signatory to the International Organization of Securities Commissions' (IOSCO) multilateral Memorandum of Understanding. Limits on individual and aggregate investment for QFIs will be 5 percent and 10 percent of the company's paid-up capital, respectively. These limits are over and above the cap earmarked for foreign institutional investors (FIIs) and non-resident individuals (NRIs), who can invest directly in the Indian equity market. Foreign Venture Capital Investors (FVCIs) need to register with SEBI to invest in Indian firms. They can also set up a domestic asset management company to manage the fund. All such investments are allowed under the automatic route, subject to SEBI and RBI regulations and FDI policy. FVCIs can invest in many sectors including software business, information technology, pharmaceutical and drugs, bio-technology, nanotechnology, biofuels, agriculture, and infrastructure. Companies incorporated outside India can raise capital in India's capital market through the issuance of Indian Depository Receipts (IDRs).

Companies are required to have pre-issue, paid-up capital and free reserves of least USD 100 million, as well as an average turnover of USD 500 million during the three financial years preceding the issuance. In addition, they must have been profitable for at least five years preceding the issue, declaring dividends of not less than 10 percent each year and maintaining a debt-equity ratio of not more than 2:1. Standard Chartered Bank, a British bank which was the first foreign entity to list in India in June 2010, is the only firm to have issued IDRs. In July 2011, a SEBI directive placed restrictions on conversion of actively traded IDRs in shares. The new SEBI directive describes illiquidity as an annualized turnover for the previous six months that is less than five percent of the total numbers of IDRs issued. External Commercial Borrowing (ECB or direct lending to Indian entities by foreign institutions and non- banking finance companies) is allowed if the funds will be used for outward FDI or domestically for investment in industry, infrastructure, hotels, hospitals, or software. ECBs may not be used for on-lending, working capital, financial assets, or acquiring real estate or a domestic firm.

Generally, any non-financial firm can borrow up to USD 500 million per year through ECBs via the automatic route. As of November 2011, the all-in-costs ceilings for ECBs with an average maturity period of three to five years was capped at 350 basis points over six month LIBOR and 500 points for loans maturing after five years. As the cost of credit is significantly less in overseas markets, Indian companies have borrowed close to USD 30.5 billion in foreign currency through ECBs and FCCBs so far in 2011, compared to borrowings of USD 19.2 billion in 2010. Takeover regulations require disclosure upon acquisition of shares exceeding five percent of total capitalization. Acquisition of 15 percent or more of the voting rights in a listed company triggers a public offer, per SEBI regulations. The public offer made by the acquiring entity (i.e., an individual, company, or other legal entity) must be for at least 20 percent of the company's voting rights. Since October 2008, an owner holding between 55 percent and 75 percent of voting rights can acquire additional voting rights of up to five percent without making a public offer (i.e., creeping acquisition). However, the buyer can make a creeping acquisition only by open market purchases and not through bulk/block/negotiated deals or preferential allotment. Furthermore, subsequent to this acquisition, the buyer's total shares should not cross the 75 percent threshold. RBI and FIPB clearances are required to assume a controlling stake in an Indian company. Cross shareholding and stable shareholding are no prevalent in the Indian market. SEBI regulates hostile takeovers.

Competition from State Owned Enterprises

India's public sector enterprises (PSEs), both at the central and state levels, play an important role in the country's industrialization. There are currently 250 Central Public Sector Enterprises (CPSEs). The manufacturing sector constitutes the largest component of investment in CPSEs (45 percent) followed by services (35 percent), electricity (12 percent), and mining (8 percent). Foreigners, including Americans, are allowed to invest in these sectors. The Ministry of Heavy Industries and Public Enterprises' Department of Public Enterprises oversees CPSEs. CPSEs have a Board of Directors, wherein at least one third of the directors should be externally appointed without being promoters or relatives of promoters. The chairman, managing director, and directors are appointed independently. Companies can appoint private consultants, senior retired officers, and politically affiliated individuals to their boards.

In December 2009, the government established the "Maharatna" status for four CPSEs, allowing them greater financial and operational freedom to expand their operations and emerge as global giants. Maharatna CPSEs are allowed to invest up to USD 1.1 billion without government approval. The four CPSEs with Maharatna status include Indian Oil Corporation, NTPC Limited, Oil and Natural Gas Corporation, and Steel Authority of India. To qualify for Maharatna status, these CPSEs established a track record of excellent financial performance for the past three years, with a turnover of at least USD 5.5 billion, a net worth of USD 3.3 billion, and profitability of USD 1.1 billion. Nineteen other CPSEs achieved "Navratna" status, which affords them the autonomy to make investment decisions up to USD 240 million without government approval. Navratna- rated CPSEs are expected to maintain a net profit of Rs 300 million or more over three years or at least in one of the three years.

The government plans to pursue disinvestment in CPSEs, but would retain at least 51 percent ownership. Americans are allowed to buy equity stakes in these Maharatna and Navratna companies via IPOs. Although there do not appear to be systemic advantages, CPSEs in some sectors enjoy pricing and bidding advantages over their private sector and foreign competitors. The government has increased its pace for reducing its equity ownership in CPSEs, although there are no plans to sell majority shares of CPSEs to the private sector or to list more than 50 percent of the shares on any of the Indian stock exchanges. India will pose challenges for these CPSEs as the leveling of the playing-field will decrease their ability to benefit from special privileges and concessions.

Corporate Social Responsibility

Awareness of corporate social responsibility (CSR) in India is growing, especially as the private sector continues to experience positive results from influencing the areas of Indian society directly linked to their business. CSR efforts by Tata Group, Wipro, and Reliance are setting examples for the rest of the Indian private sector. U.S. companies are also doing their part, with an Indian-based U.S. company, Cargill, being named a finalist in the Secretary of State's 2011 Award for Corporate Excellence. As a regular practice, CSR is not as widely found among SMEs in India. In July 2011, the Ministry of Corporate Affairs released its "National Voluntary Guidelines on Social, Environmental & Economic Responsibilities of Business." These replaced April 2010 guidelines requiring Central Public Sector Enterprises (CPSE) to spend 0.5 percent to 5 percent of their net profits on CSR activities, as well as watered-down follow-up guidelines, announced in December 2010, which said companies need only adopt a policy showing how they would spend two percent of their profits on CSR and, if they did spend the money, disclose how they did so.

Political Violence

There were no reported politically motivated attacks on U.S. companies operating in India in 2011. There were protests in Andhra Pradesh, which led to strikes and violence over the carving out of a new state of Telangana from Andhra Pradesh.

There continue to be outbursts of violence related to insurgent movements in Jammu and Kashmir and similar events in some northeastern states. Maoist/Naxalite insurgent groups remain active in some eastern and central Indian states, including the rural areas of Bihar, Jharkhand, Chhattisgarh, West Bengal, and Orissa.

Corruption

The anti-corruption movement has dominated Parliamentary sessions, media, and public debate, as the government seeks to pass a national ombudsman law in response to the Anna Hazare-led anti-corruption movement. Increasingly, the middle class is gathering its voice against the type of scandals seen in the 2010 Commonwealth Games, the sale of the 2G spectrum, and everyday petty corruption. India's ranking in Transparency International's Corruption Perception Index slipped in 2011, to 95 out of 183 countries surveyed from the previous year's ranking of 87 out of 178 countries. In the 2010 Global Corruption Barometer survey, also by Transparency International, 54 percent of respondents in India said they had paid a bribe in the past 12 months. That puts India ninth after Liberia (89 percent), Uganda (86 percent), Cambodia (84 percent), Sierra Leone (71 percent), Nigeria (63 percent), Afghanistan (61 percent), Iraq, and Senegal (both at 56 percent).

Media coverage of corruption cases is expected to continue to dominate the press for the coming months. The high profile cases that are troubling the government include questionable kickbacks on Commonwealth Games construction contracts, land development schemes in Maharashtra and Karnataka, and the dubious allocation of telecom licenses. The legal framework for fighting corruption is addressed by the following laws: the Prevention of Corruption Act, 1988; the Code of Criminal Procedures, 1973; the Companies Act, 1956; the Indian Contract Act, 1872; and the Prevention of Money Laundering Act, 2002. Anti-corruption laws amended since 2004, granted additional powers to vigilance departments in government ministries and PSEs at the central and state levels and made the Central Vigilance Commission (CVC) a statutory body. In May 2011, the GOI ratified the United Nations Convention against Corruption.

The Prime Minister has set an ambitious Parliamentary agenda to pass legislation intended to curb corruption. His arsenal includes a bill to protect whistleblowers, a government procurement bill, amendments to increase and expand the prevention of money laundering act, and a bill to channel grievances against poor delivery of government services. The national Right to Information Act, 2005, and equivalent state acts function similarly to the U.S. Freedom of Information Act, requiring government officials to furnish information requested by citizens or face punitive action. The increased computerization of services, coupled with central and state government efforts to establish vigilance commissions, is opening up avenues to seek redress for grievances.

In November 2010, then-Corporate Affairs Minister Salman Khurshid said the government may review the act's scope to ensure greater transparency in corporate lobbying. This would require Parliamentary approval and hence may take some time.

U.S. firms continue to identify corruption as a major obstacle to FDI, citing lack of transparency in the rules of governance, extremely cumbersome official procedures, and excessive and unregulated discretionary power in the hands of politicians and bureaucrats.

U.S. Foreign Corrupt Practices Act: In 1977, the United States enacted the Foreign Corrupt Practices Act (FCPA), which makes it unlawful for a U.S. person, and certain foreign issuers of securities, to make a corrupt payment to foreign public officials for the purpose of obtaining or retaining business for or with, or directing business to, any person. The FCPA also applies to foreign firms and persons who take any act in furtherance of such a corrupt payment while in the United States. OECD Antibribery Convention: The OECD Antibribery Convention entered into force in February 1999. As of March 2009, there are 38 parties to the Convention including the United States. Major exporters China, India, and Russia are not parties, although the U.S. Government strongly endorses their eventual accession to the Convention. The Convention obligates the Parties to criminalize bribery of foreign public officials in the conduct of international business. The United States meets its international obligations under the OECD Antibribery Convention through the U.S. FCPA. India is not a party to the OECD.

UN Convention: The UN Anticorruption Convention entered into force on December 14, 2005, and there are 158 parties to it as of November 2011. The UN Convention is the first global comprehensive international anticorruption agreement. The UN Convention requires countries to establish criminal and other offences to cover a wide range of acts of corruption. The UN Convention goes beyond previous anticorruption instruments, covering a broad range of issues ranging from basic forms of corruption such as bribery and solicitation, embezzlement, trading in influence to the concealment and laundering of the proceeds of corruption. The Convention contains transnational business bribery provisions that are functionally similar to those in the OECD Antibribery Convention and contains provisions on private sector auditing and books and records requirements. Other provisions address matters such as prevention, international cooperation, and asset recovery. India signed the agreement in 2005 and ratified the agreement in 2011.

Local Laws: U.S. firms should familiarize themselves with local anticorruption laws, and, where appropriate, seek legal counsel. While the U.S. Department of Commerce cannot provide legal advice on local laws, the Department's U.S. and Foreign Commercial Service can provide assistance with navigating the host country's legal system and obtaining a list of local legal counsel.

Assistance for U.S. Businesses: The U.S. Department of Commerce offers several services to aid U.S. businesses seeking to address business-related corruption issues. For example, the U.S. and Foreign Commercial Service can provide services that may assist U.S. companies in conducting their due diligence as part of the company's overarching compliance program when choosing business partners or agents overseas. The Departments of Commerce and State provide worldwide support for qualified U.S. companies bidding on foreign government contracts through the Commerce Department's Advocacy Center and State's Office of Commercial and Business Affairs. Problems, including alleged corruption by foreign governments or competitors, encountered by U.S. companies in seeking such foreign business opportunities can be brought to the attention of appropriate U.S. government officials, including local embassy personnel and through the Department of Commerce Trade Compliance Center "Report A Trade Barrier."

Guidance on the U.S. FCPA: The Department of Justice's (DOJ) FCPA Opinion Procedure enables U.S. firms and individuals to request a statement of the Justice Department's present enforcement intentions under the anti-bribery provisions of the FCPA regarding any proposed business conduct. Although the Department of Commerce has no enforcement role with respect to the FCPA, it supplies general guidance to U.S. exporters who have questions about the FCPA and about international developments concerning the FCPA. Exporters and investors should be aware that generally all countries prohibit the bribery of their public officials, and prohibit their officials from soliciting bribes under domestic laws.

Bilateral Investment Agreements

As of December 2010, India concluded 76 bilateral investment agreements, including with the United Kingdom, France, Germany, Switzerland, Malaysia, and Mauritius. In 2009, India concluded a Comprehensive Economic Cooperation Agreement (CEPA) with ASEAN and a free trade agreement (FTA) in goods, services, and investment with South Korea. In February 2011, India signed CEPAs with Japan and Malaysia. FTA negotiations with the EU and Canada are still under way and India is negotiating a CEPA with Thailand. India is also keen to engage the United States in a Bilateral Investment Treaty (BIT) or Comprehensive Economic Partnership Agreement (CEPA). The United States and India resumed technical discussions towards a Bilateral Investment Treaty (BIT) in October 2011. India continues to express interest in negotiating a social security totalization agreement with the United States. It already has totalization agreements with Belgium, France, Germany, Switzerland, the Netherlands, Hungary, the Czech Republic, Denmark, Luxembourg, and Canada. The U.S. Department of Commerce's International Trade Administration's "Invest in America" program and "Invest India," a joint venture between DIPP and the Federation of Indian Chambers of Commerce and Industry, signed a Memorandum of Intent in November 2009, to facilitate FDI in both countries. India and the United States already have a double taxation avoidance treaty. Several tax disputes are pending that are being addressed during regular meetings between the two countries' competent authorities.

OPIC and Other Investment Insurance Programs

The United States and India signed an Investment Incentive Agreement in 1987, which covers Overseas Private Investment Corporate (OPIC) programs. OPIC is currently operating in India in the areas of renewable energy and power, telecommunications, manufacturing, housing, services, and education, and plans to invest more than USD 212 million dollars in 2011, in clean energy and energy efficiency projects. India is a member of the World Bank's Multilateral Investment Guarantee Agency (MIGA). The Export-Import Bank of the United States has also increased its activities in India, which is now Ex-Im's second largest market after Mexico.

Labor

Although there are more than seven million unionized workers in India, unions represent less than one- seventh of the workers in the formal economy – primarily state entities – and less than two percent of the total work force. Most unions are linked to political parties. According to provisional figures from the Ministry of Labor, 17.9 million work-days were lost to strikes and lockouts during 2010, as opposed to 13.5 million work-days lost in 2009. Labor unrest occurs throughout India, though the reasons and affected sectors vary widely.

In 2011, foreign companies in the manufacturing sector, such as General Motors, experienced labor problems in Gujarat, while others in the same sector report excellent labor relations. Some labor problems are the result of workplace disagreements, including pay, working conditions, and union representation, but other unrest may be related to local political conditions beyond the companies' control. The states of Gujarat, Kerala, Andhra Pradesh, Karnataka, and Rajasthan experience the most strikes and lockouts, according to government statistics. Sectors with the most labor unrest include banks, excluding insurance and pension, and the automobile industry.

As of December 2011, the GOI continues to consult with state governments on ratifying the International Labor Organization (ILO) convention promoting worker rights in terms of health and safety in mining operations. Interest peaked in this issue when trade unions representing miners in November 2009, urged the government to ratify the convention. It is a commonly held belief throughout India that accidents are under- reported. India's labor regulations are among the world's most stringent and complex, and they limit the growth of the formal manufacturing sector. The payment of wages is governed by the Payment of Wages Act, 1936, and the Minimum Wages Act, 1948. Industrial wages vary by state, ranging from about USD 3.50 per day for unskilled workers to over USD 150 per month for skilled production workers. Retrenchment, closure, and layoffs are governed by the Industrial Disputes Act, 1947, which requires prior government permission to lay off workers or close businesses employing more than 100 people. Permission is not easily obtained, resulting in a high use of contract workers in the manufacturing sector to circumvent the law.

Private firms successfully downsize through voluntary retirement schemes. Foreign banks also require RBI approval to close branches. In August 2010, Parliament passed the Industrial Disputes (Amendment) Bill, 2010, which contains several provisions that: increase the wage ceiling prescribed for supervisors; bring disputes between contractors and contracted labor under the purview of the Ministry of Labor in consultation with relevant state or central government offices; provide direct access for workers to labor courts or tribunals in case of disputes; seek more qualified officers to preside over labor courts or tribunals; establish a grievance process; and empower industrial tribunals-cum-courts to enforce decrees.

Foreign-Trade Zones/Free Ports

The GOI established several foreign trade zone schemes to encourage export-oriented production. These include Special Economic Zones (SEZ), Export Processing Zones (EPZ), Software Technology Parks (STP), and Export Oriented Units (EOU). SEZs are treated as foreign territory, allowing businesses operating in SEZs to operate outside the domain of the customs authorities, avoid FDI equity caps, receive exemptions from industrial licensing requirements, and enjoy tax holidays and other tax breaks. Land acquisition concerns have led to restrictions in developing SEZs. EPZs are industrial parks with incentives for foreign investors in export-oriented businesses. STPs are special zones with similar incentives for software exports. Both receive breaks on customs duties. Export Oriented Units (EOUs) are industrial companies established anywhere in India that export their entire production. They are granted: duty-free import of intermediate goods; income tax holidays; exemption from excise tax on capital goods, components, and raw materials; and a waiver of sales taxes.

Chapter 8: Trade and Project Financing

Methods of Payment

Import financing procedures adhere to western business practices. The safest method of receiving payments is through an irrevocable letter of credit (L/C). The L/C should be payable in favor of the supplier against presentation of shipping documents through the importer's bank. Importers open L/C's valid for three to six months depending upon the terms of the agreement. Typically L/C's are opened for a period of time to cover production and shipping, and they are normally paid within seven working days of the receipt of goods. There are several lines of credit available to U.S companies.

The most important source for finance for the corporate sector continues to be the capital markets. Companies are not required to obtain prior permission from the GOI to access capital markets, but it is compulsory for companies to obtain Reserve Bank of India's permission before issuing any shares to a non-resident investor. Indian companies can also issue American Depository Receipts (ADR) and Global Depository Receipts (GDR) without any value limits. Several steps have been taken to improve liquidity in the ADR / GDR market abroad. Indian companies are increasingly accessing overseas markets to raise finances through these instruments. Commercial banks continue to be the main source of short-term finance and working capital requirements of Indian firms.

Indian Companies also raise funds by issuing commercial paper and debentures, from inter- corporate borrowings, and by accepting public deposits. Several term-lending public financial institutions provide local and foreign exchange loans for new capital investment projects. They also provide deferred payment loans, long-term working capital finance, export credit and stock underwriting services. Lending banks secure their loans with company assets, corporate guarantees from a parent company, and, in some cases, by personal guarantees from company directors. Local and resident foreign companies are permitted to raise medium-to-long-term loans in foreign currency for projects requiring capital equipment, technology imports, or the purchase of aircraft or ships.

The Indian government permits borrowing through suppliers' credits, buyers' credits, syndicated loans, floating-rate notes, revolving underwriting facilities and bonds. The RBI permits loans, which mature within one year, to be repaid from net foreign exchange earnings without prior government approval. Loans in foreign currencies can be obtained through foreign commercial banks, overseas financial institutions (e.g., the International Finance Corporation and the Asian Development Bank), and foreign export-credit agencies, in addition to Indian development and commercial banks. Indian companies can also raise foreign currency loans in accordance with the guidelines for External Commercial Borrowings (ECB's), issued by the Ministry of Finance. There are no restrictions on the use of such loans, except that they cannot be used for stock market speculation. Once the RBI and Ministry of Finance have approved a loan and its terms, no limitations are placed on interest and principal payments. A firm, however, must report to the RBI through its designated banker every time an interest payment is made.

How Does the Banking System Operate

India has an extensive banking network, in both urban and rural areas. The banking system has three tiers. These are: the scheduled commercial banks; the regional rural banks, which operate in rural areas, not covered by the scheduled banks; and the cooperative and special purpose rural banks. Timely availability of adequate credit is of utmost importance for the development of the Indian rural economy and agriculture. At present Regional Rural Banks, commercial banks and credit cooperatives, encouraged mainly by the Government of India (GOI), undertake this function. The GOI, during the recent budget, announced that it would encourage private banks to open branches in rural areas, to service both farm and non-farm sectors.

There are approximately 80 scheduled commercial banks, Indian and foreign; almost 200 regional rural banks; more than 350 central cooperative banks, 20 land development banks; and a number of primary agricultural credit societies. Large Indian banks and most Indian financial institutions are in the public sector. Though public sector banks (27 of them) currently dominate the banking industry, numerous private and foreign banks exist. Several public sector banks are being restructured, and in some cases the government either has already reduced, or is in the process of reducing its ownership. In terms of business, the state-owned banks account for more than 70 percent of deposits and loans. Private banks handle 17 percent of the market, and foreign banks located in metropolitan area account for approximately 13 percent of the market.

The Reserve Bank of India (RBI) is the central banking institution. It is the sole authority for issuing bank notes and the supervisory body for banking operations in India. It supervises and administers exchange control and banking regulations, and administers the government's monetary policy. It is also responsible for granting licenses for new bank branches. The Deposit Insurance and Credit Guarantee Corporation, an organization promoted and fully funded by the RBI, offers deposit insurance facilities. The RBI directs banks to meet Bureau of Indian Standards guidelines. Indian banks must also adhere to the prudential norms laid down by the Basel Group. The Reserve Bank of India (RBI) also sets India's exchange-control policy and administers foreign exchange regulations in consultation with the GOI. India's foreign exchange control regime is governed by the FEMA (Foreign Exchange Management Act), enacted with the objective of facilitating external trade and payments and for promoting the orderly development and maintenance of foreign exchange market in India, and to give effect to the liberalization announced in the economic policies.

The Export-Import Bank (Ex-Im Bank) is the official export credit agency of the United States and supports the purchase of U.S. goods and services by creditworthy Indian buyers that may have difficulty obtaining credit through traditional financing sources. Ex-Im Bank provides U.S. exporters with the financing tools they need to successfully compete for business in India. Ex-Im Bank support gives protection against international political and commercial risk, and gives U.S. exporters the ability to offer competitive financing to their Indian buyers through export credit insurance and loan guarantees. Over the past 70 years, Ex-Im Bank has supported more than $400 billion of U.S. exports worldwide.

OPIC is an independent U.S. government agency whose mission is to mobilize and facilitate the participation of U. S. private capital and skills in the economic and social development of less developed countries and areas, and countries in transition from non-market to market economies. OPIC assists U.S. companies by providing financing (from large structured finance to small business loans), political risk insurance, and investment funds. OPIC complements the private sector in managing risks associated with foreign direct investment and supports U.S. foreign policy. OPIC was established as an agency of the U.S. government in 1971 and currently does business in over 150 countries.

The U.S. Trade and Development Agency (USTDA) advances economic development and U.S. commercial interests in developing and middle income countries. The agency funds various forms of technical assistance, feasibility studies, training, orientation visits and business workshops that support the development of a modern infrastructure and a fair and open trading environment. USTDA's strategic use of foreign assistance funds to support sound investment policy and decision-making in host countries creates an enabling environment for trade, investment and sustainable economic development. Operating at the nexus of foreign policy and commerce, USTDA is uniquely positioned to work with U.S. firms and host countries in achieving the agency's trade and development goals. In carrying out its mission, USTDA gives emphasis to economic sectors that may benefit from U.S. exports of goods and services.

Asia's premier non-profit financial institution, the Asian Development Bank (ADB), is headquartered in Manila, Philippines. The ADB's major objective is the promotion of the social and economic well being of its developing member countries in Asia and the Pacific. This is achieved by lending funds to projects involving agriculture, energy, industry, transportation, and communication, as well as for social infrastructure projects such as water supply, sewage and sanitation, education, health and urban development. The ADB also invests in, and lends to, the private sector for Build-Own-Operate (BOO) and Build-Operate-Transfer (BOT) infrastructure, industrial and capital market development projects and mobilizes additional resources through co-financing arrangements, including the bank's credit enhancement instruments such as guarantees and complementary financing plans.

The U.S. Department of Commerce maintains a Congressionally mandated Commercial Liaison Office for the ADB (CS ADB). The Office's mission is to help American firms access, enter and expand in Asian markets that benefit from ADB assistance. The office provides counseling, advocacy, project information, and conducts outreach programs in the region as well as in the U.S.

to help U.S. firms take advantage of commercial opportunities in countries borrowing from the ADB.To perform its mandate, the office cooperates with the U.S. Director's Office at ADB and works closely with Commercial Service posts in the region. An American Senior Commercial Officer heads the office, assisted by two Commercial Specialists.

The World Bank Group is one of the world's largest sources of development assistance. The World Bank supports the efforts of developing country governments to build schools and health centers, provide water and electricity, fight disease, and protect the environment. The "World Bank" is the name that has come to be used for the International Bank for Reconstruction and Development (IBRD) and the International Development Association (IDA). Together these organizations provide low-interest loans, interest-free credit, and grants to developing countries.

The World Bank's New Delhi office has an active public information center with a large collection of World Bank and other publications on India and international development, and documents on projects financed by the Bank. In recent years, the World Bank's IBRD has been giving support for India's economic policy reforms and expanded social and environmental programs. The U.S. Department of Commerce maintains a Commercial Liaison Office at the World Bank. The Office's mission is to help American firms access, enter and expand in markets that benefit from World Bank assistance. The office provides counseling, advocacy, project information, and conducts outreach programs in the region as well as in the U.S.

to help U.S. firms take advantage of commercial opportunities in countries borrowing from the World Bank.

The International Finance Corporation (IFC) promotes sustainable private sector investment in developing countries as a way to reduce poverty and improve people's lives. IFC is a member of the World Bank Group and is headquartered in Washington, DC. It shares the primary objective of all World Bank Group institutions: to improve the quality of the lives of people in its developing member countries. Established in 1956, IFC is the largest multilateral source of loan and equity financing for private sector projects in the developing world. It promotes sustainable private sector development primarily by financing private sector projects located in the developing world; helping private companies in the developing world mobilize financing in international financial markets; providing advice and technical assistance to businesses and governments.

Although the IFC coordinates its activities in many areas with the other institutions in the World Bank Group, the IFC generally operates independently as it is legally and financially autonomous with its own Articles of Agreement, share capital, management and staff.The IFC fosters sustainable economic growth in developing countries by financing private sector investment, mobilizing capital in the international financial markets, and providing advisory services to businesses and governments.

MIGA, a member of the World Bank group, supplements the activities of the IBRD (International Bank for Reconstruction and Development), IFC and other international development finance institutions. It complements the activities of national and regional development insurance through co-insurance and reinsurance agreements with these institutions, bilateral exchanges of information, and its membership in the Berne Union. MIGA issues guarantees against noncommercial risks for investments in its developing member countries. MIGA guarantees cover the following risks: currency transfer, expropriation, war and civil disturbance and breach of contract by a host government. Since its inception in 1988, MIGA has issued nearly 800 guarantees worth more than $14.7 billion for projects in 91 developing countries. MIGA is committed to promoting socially, economically, and environmentally sustainable projects that are above all, developmentally responsible. The agency mobilizes additional investment coverage through its Cooperative Underwriting Program (CUP), encouraging private sector insurers into transactions they would not have otherwise undertaken, and helping the agency serve more clients.

Chapter 9: Contacts

The U.S. Commercial Service India Senior Commercial Officer is: Judy R. Reinke:

judy@reinke@trade.gov

U.S. Embassy
The American Center
24, Kasturba Gandhi Marg
Connaught Place
New Delhi 110 0001
Tel: 91-11-2347 2000; 2419-8000
Fax: 91-11-2331-5172

Deputy Senior Commercial Officer: Margaret Hanson-Muse
margaret.hanson-muse@trade.gov

Principal Commercial Officer: Greg O'Connor
greg.o'connor@trade.gov

Commercial Officer: Pat Cassidy
pat.cassidy@trade.gov

Commercial Officer: Olga Ford
olga.ford@trade.gov

U.S. Patent and Trade Office (USPTO)
IPR Attaché: Kalpana Reddy
kalpana.reddy@trade.gov

Bureau of Industry and Security (BIS)

Export Control Officer: Perry Davis

perry.davis@trade.gov

U.S. Commercial Service Mumbai

American Consulate General

American Center

4 New Marine Lines

Mumbai 400 020

Tel: 91-22-2265-2511

Fax: 91-22-2262-3850

Principal Commercial Officer: Richard Rothman

richard.rothman@trade.gov

U.S. Commercial Service Chennai

American Consulate General

220 Mount Road, Chennai 600 006

Tel: 91-44-2857 4191/4477

Fax: 91-44-2857 4212

Principal Commercial Officer: James Golsen

james.golsen@trade.gov

U.S. Commercial Service Kolkata

American Consulate General

American Center

38-A, Jawaharlal Nehru Road

Kolkata 700071

Tel: 91-33- 3984 6300

Fax: 91-33- 2288 1207

Principal Commercial Officer: Richard Craig
richard.craig@trade.gov

U.S. Commercial Service Bangalore
The Commercial Service
S2, II Floor, Red Cross Bhawan
No. 26, Racecourse Road
Bangalore 560001
Tel: 91-80-220-6404; Fax: 91-80-220-6405
Commercial Specialist: Leonard Roberts
leonard.roberts@trade.gov

U.S. Commercial Service Ahmedabad
The Commercial Service
401/402, JMC House
Ambawadi, Near Parimal Garden
Ahmedabad 380 006
Tel: 91-79-2656 5210/16
Fax: 91-79-2656 0763
Commercial Specialist: Sangeeta Taneja
sangeeta.taneja@trade.gov

U.S. Commercial Service Hyderabad
The Commercial Service
Taj Residency Hotel
#555, E Level,
Road No. 1, Banjara Hills, Hyderabad 500 034
Tel: 91-40-23305000, 23393939
Fax: 91-40-23300130
Commercial Specialist: Radhakishore Pandrangi

pandrangi.radhakishore@trade.gov

Chambers of Commerce

Ms. Nivedita Mehra

Program Director, India

U.S.-India Business Council

nmehra@uschamber.com

12 Hailey Road

New Delhi 110001 INDIA

Mr. Ajay Singha, Executive Director

American Chamber of Commerce in India (AMCHAM)

PHD House, 4th Floor,

4/2, Siri Institutional Area,

August Kranti Marg,

New Delhi -110016 Tel : 91-11-2652 5201/ 2652 5202

Fax : 91-11-2652 5203

Email : amcham@amchamindia.com

Mr. Chandrajit Banerjee,

Director General

Confederation of Indian Industry (CII)

The Mantosh Sondhi Centre

23, Institutional Area, Lodi Road

New Delhi 110003, India

Tel: +91-11-2462-9994-7

Fax: +91-11-2463-3168; 2462-6149

Email: ciico@ciionline.org

http://www.ciionline.org

Dr. Rajiv Kumar

Secretary General

Federation of Indian Chambers of Commerce & Industry (FICCI)

Federation House, Tansen Marg

New Delhi 110001, India

Tel: +91-11-2373-8760-70

Direct: +91-11-2335-7364

Fax: +91-11-2372-1504; 2332-0714

Email: rkumar@ficci.com

http://www.ficci.com

Mr. Atul Vyas,

Regional Director

Indo-American Chamber of Commerce (IACC)

PHD House (4th Floor), Opp. Asian Games Village

New Delhi 110 016

Tel: +91-11-26963387, 26531965, 26518201

Fax: +91-11-26531954

Email: indo-american@eth.net

http://www.iaccindia.com

Mr. D. S. Rawat

Secretary General

The Associated Chambers of Commerce

& Industry of India (ASSOCHAM)

ASSOCHAM Corporate Office, 1, Community Centre

Zamrudpur, Kailash Colony, New Delhi – 110 048

Tel: +91-11- 46550555

Fax: +91-11-46536481/46536482 46536497/46536498

E-mail: assocham@nic.in

http://www.assocham.org

Ms. Susmita Shekhar
Secretary General
Email : sshekhar@phdcci.in
PHD Chamber of Commerce & Industry
PHD House,
4/2 Siri Institutional Area
August Kranti Marg, New Delhi 110016
Phone: 91-11-26863801-4, 26866814, 26857745-46
Fax: 91-11-26855450, 26863135
E-mail: phdcci@phdcci.in
http://www.phdcci.in

Dr. Atindra Sen
Director General
Bombay Chamber of Commerce & Industry
Mackinnon Mackenzie Building, 3rd Floor
Ballard Estate, Mumbai-400001
Tel: +91-22-2261-4681
Fax: +91-22-2262-1213
E-Mail: bcci@bombaychamber.com
http://www.bombaychamber.com

Ms. Bhavana Doshi,
President,
Indian Merchants' Chamber, IMC Building
Indian Merchants' Chamber Marg
Churchgate
Mumbai-400020

Tel: +91-22-2204-6633, 2204-1919

Fax: +91-22-2204-8508, 2283-8281

Email: imc@imcnet.org

http://www.incnet.org

Trade Associations

Mr. Som Mittal

President

National Association of Software

and Service Companies (NASSCOM)

International Youth Centre

Teen Murti Marg

Chanakyapuri

New Delhi - 110021, India

Tel: +91-11-2301-0199

Fax: +91-11-2331- 5452

Website: http://www.nasscom.org

Dr Alok Bharadwaj,

President

Manufacturers' Association

for Information Technology (MAIT)

PHD House, 4th Floor

Opp. Asian Games Village

New Delhi 110 016, India

Tel: +91-11-2685-5487; 2685-4284; 2687-6976

Fax: +91-11-2685-1321

E-mail: mait@vsnl.com

Website: http://www.mait.com

Mr. Vikram Sirur

President

Indian Machine Tool Manufacturers' Association (IMTMA)

Plot 249 F, Phase IV, Udyog Vihar, Sector 18

Gurgaon 122 015, Haryana (INDIA)

Phone: +91-124-4014101/2/3/4

Fax: +91-124-4014108

Email: imtmahq@vsnl.in, imtma@del2.vsnl.net.in

http://www.imtma.in

Mr. Vinnie Mehta

Executive Director

Automotive Component Manufacturers

Association of India (ACMA)

6th Floor the Capital Court,

Olof Palme Marg, Munirka,

New Delhi 110 067.

Tel.: +91 11 2616 0315, 2617 5873, 2618 4479

Fax: +91 11 2616 0317

E-mail: acma@vsnl.com, acma@vsnl.net

http://www.acmainfo.com

Mr. Rajnish Joshi

President - India Chapter

American Society of Heating, Refrigerating and

Airconditioning Engineers (ASHRAE) and

Indian Society of Heating, Refrigerating and

Airconditioning Engineers (ISHRAE)

K-43 Kailash Colony (Basement)

New Delhi 110048, India

Tel: +91-11-416-35655

Fax: +91-11-29234925

E-mail: ashraeic@touchtelindia.net

http://www.ashraeindia.org

Mr. Cherian Varkey

President

Builders Association of India

G-I/G 20 Commerce Centre 7th Floor

J. Dadajee Road Tardeo

Mumbai 400034, India

Tel: +91-22-2351-4134, 2351-4802

Fax: +91-22-2352-0507

Email: baihq.mumbai@gmail.com, baidelhi16@gmail.com.

http://www.baionline.in/

Mr. Sanjeev Joshi

Executive Director

Project Exports Promotion Council of India

H-118, Himalaya House, 11th Floor

23 Kasturba Gandhi Marg

New Delhi 110 001, India

Tel: +91-11-2373-8377; 2372-2425

Fax: +91-11-2331-2936

E-mail: info@projectsexports.com

http://www.projectexports.com

Mr. Manish U. Doshi

President

Indian Drug Manufacturers Association (IDMA)

102 B Poonam Chambers, A Wing, First Floor

Dr. A. Besant Road, Worli

Mumbai 400 018, India

Tel: +91-22-2497-4308, 2494-4624

Fax: +91-22-2495-0723

Email: idma1@idmaindia.com, idma_del1@redifmail.com

http://www.idma-assn.org

Mr. Ramesh Chandak

President

Indian Electrical & Electronics

Manufacturers Association (IEEMA)

501 Kakad Chambers - 5th Floor

132 Dr. Annie Besant Road, Worli

Mumbai 400 018, India

Tel: +91-22-2493-0532/6528/6529

Fax: +91-22-2493-2705

Email: mumbai@ieema.org

http://www.ieema.org

Mr. Ranjit Shahani

President

Organization of Pharmaceutical Producers of India (OPPI)

Peninsula Chambers, Ground Floor,

Ganpatrao Kadam Marg,

Lower Parel,

Mumbai 400 013

Tel: +91-22-24918123, 24912486, 56627007

Fax: +91-22-24915168

Email: indiaoppi@vsnl.com

http://www.indiaoppi.com

Dr S Chatterjee

President

Consulting Engineers Association of India

OCF Plot No.2, Pocket 9, Sector – B,

(Behind Jagannath Institute of Management Studies)

Vasant Kunj, New Delhi 110070

Tel: 91-11- 26134644,

Telefax: 91-11- 26139658

E-mail: ceai.ceai@gmail.com

Website: www.ceaindia.org

Professor S.K. Brahmachari

Chairman

Consultancy Development Centre

East Court, Zone 4, Core 4B

2nd Floor, India Habitat Center

Lodi Road

New Delhi 110 003

Tel: +91-11-2460-2915, 24601533, 2464-8268(D)

Fax: +91-11-2460-2602

E-mail: cdc@vsnl.com

http://www.cdc.org.in

Mr. Gurpal Singh

Deputy Director General

National Committee on Defense

Confederation of Indian Industry

India Habitat Centre

4th Floor, Core 4A, Lodi Road

New Delhi - 110 003, India

Tel: +91 11 41504514 - 19

Fax: +91 11 24682229

Website: http://www.ciidefence.com

U.S. Banks and Local Correspondent Banks

American Express Bank Ltd.

Mr. Rajesh Saxena

Chief Executive Officer

Cyber City, tower C/8

DLF City Phase II, Sector 25

Gurgaon 122002, Haryana

Telephone: 91-0124-4190555; Fax: 91-0124-2801144

Bank of America

Mr. Kevin Watts

Managing Director and Country Manager

Express Towers

16th Floor, Nariman Point

Mumbai 400 021

Telephone: 91-22-2285 2882

Fax: 91-22-2202 9016

J.P. Morgan Chase

Ms. Kalpana Morparia

Chief Executive Officer

Mafatlal Center, 9th Floor

Nariman Point, Mumbai 400 021, India

Telephone: 91-22- 2281-6110 (D); 2281 7645

Fax: 91-22-22855666 (D)

Citibank N.A.

Mr. Pramit Jhaveri

City Country Officer

Citi Center, 5th Floor, Plot C-61

G Block, Bandra Kurla Complex

Bandra (East), Mumbai 400 051, India

Telephone: 91-22-2653-5858; 4001 5015(D)

Fax: 91-22-2653-5859

Email: sanjay.nayar@citi.com

Lending Institutions

Mr. Robert Drumheller

Vice President of Structured Finance

Overseas Private Investment Corporation

1100 New York Avenue, N.W.

Washington, DC 20527

Tel: 202-336-8700

Fax: 202-336-7949

Website: http://www.opic.gov

Ms. Talaat Rahman

Business Development, India

Export-Import Bank of the United States

811 Vermont Avenue, N.W., Office 911

Washington, DC 20571

Tel: 202-565-3911

Fax: 202-565-3931

Website: http://www.exim.gov

Mr. Henry Steingass

Regional Director

U.S. Trade and Development Agency

1000 Wilson Boulevard, Suite-1600

Arlington, VA 22209 - 2131

Tel: 703-875-4357

Fax: 703-875-4009

Website: http://www.tda.gov

Regional MBD/IFI Offices

Mr. Hun Kim

Country Director- India

Asian Development Bank

4, San Martin Marg

P.O. Box 5331, Chanakyapuri

New Delhi 110 021, India

Tel: 91-11-24107200

Fax: 91-11-26870955

E-mail: adbinrm@adb.org

Website: http://beta.adb.org/countries/india/contacts

Mr. Joel Fischl

Senior Commercial Officer

U.S. Commercial Liaison Office for ADB (CS/ADB)

American Business Center

25th Floor, Ayala Life-FGU Building

6811 Ayala Avenue,

Makati City, Metro Manila 1226

Philippines

Tel: 63-2- 887-1345

Fax: 63-2- 887-1164

Email: manila.adb.office@trade.gov

ADB North American Representative Office

815 Connecticut Ave, NW

Suite 325, Washington, D.C. 20006

Tel: 202-728-1500

Fax: 202-728-1505

http://www.adb.org

Email: naro@.adb.org

Mr. Paolo Martelli

Director- South Asia

International Finance Corporation

50-M, Shantipath Gate No 3, Niti Marg

Chanakyapuri

New Delhi 110 021

Tel: 91-11-4111 1000

Fax: 91-11-4111 1001

Email: southasia@ifc.org

Mr. Sudip Mozumder

Operations Advisor

The World Bank

70 Lodi Estate

New Delhi 110 003

Tel: 91-11-2461-7241

Fax: 91-11-2461-9393

Email: smozumder@worldbank.org

http://www.worldbank.org

David Fulton

Advisor & Director of Business Liaison to the World Bank

Office of the U.S. Executive Director

U.S. Trade Advocacy Center

E-mail: david.fulton@trade.gov

Phone: (202) 458-0120

Fax: (202) 477-2967

The Internationalist

www.internationalist.com